MW00830228

How to Start A Nonprofit That Will Change the World

A Comprehensive Guide to Assist Founders in Navigating the Hidden Obstacles of Building & Leading a New Nonprofit Organization

May L. Harris, Esq., M.A

Nonprofit Counsel Press
Laramie, Wyoming, USA

Copyright © 2023 by Complete Charity, LLC (dba Nonprofit Counsel).

All rights reserved. No part of this publication may be reproduced, distributed or transmitted in any form or by any means, including photocopying, recording, or other electronic or mechanical methods, without the prior written permission of the publisher, except in the case of brief quotations embodied in critical reviews and certain other noncommercial uses permitted by copyright law. For permission requests, write to the publisher, addressed "Attention: Permissions Coordinator," at the address below.

Nonprofit Counsel
213 S. 2nd Street
Laramie, WY 82070
United States of America
www.NonprofitCounsel.com

Ordering Information:
Quantity sales. Special discounts are available on quantity purchases by corporations, nonprofit organizations, associations, and others. For details contact the "Sales Department" at the address above.

Table of Contents

"It's rare to have an attorney who is not only well-versed in nonprofit corporation law, but also experienced in the nuts and bolts of navigating the challenges that come with leading a nonprofit."

Pat Libby, author, **The Empowered Citizens Guide: 10 Steps to Passing a Law that Matters to You!**

"This amazing book on how to start a successful nonprofit packs more know-how and guidance than most law books!

May Harris does an incredible job of breaking down the complexities into easy to understand steps that help a reader navigate and avoid the many pitfalls that plague nonprofits."

Kristen David, author, **Uplevel Your Business, Uplevel Your Life! 4 Pillars of Successful Business Management**

Introduction

From the Author:

It is my hope that "*How to Start a Nonprofit That Will Change the World*" will be more than just a compilation of facts and strategies for you.

It is my intent that this book will facilitate your learning, and will be a testament to the power of the passion, dedication, and collective action that you will utilize in creating lasting positive change. Drawing from my own personal experiences of starting a nonprofit from scratch, serving on various nonprofit boards of directors, and advising countless organizations, I aim to combine the theoretical knowledge I have gained with practical, real-world advice that will empower you as an aspiring nonprofit leader to navigate the complexities of establishing and managing your own organization.

I have been in your shoes, and I understand the unique challenges and complexities you may encounter. It is my sincere hope that this book will serve as a guiding light throughout your nonprofit journey.

From the initial stages of defining your mission and charting your strategic course, to the practical aspects of securing funding, assembling a committed team, and effectively measuring your impact, you will find guidance and insights that reflect the real-world challenges and triumphs of being a nonprofit founder.

Once we've completed our journey together, you will be well-prepared to start a new organization that will thrive. Whether your nonprofit aims to address environmental issues, promote education, advocate for social justice, or tackle any other pressing community need, it is my hope that this resource will continue to serve as your compass and be an ongoing source of inspiration.

Starting a nonprofit that will change the world is no easy task, but it is a goal that is within your reach. I am honored to share the knowledge I have gained over the years, and I believe this book will empower you to transform your dreams into tangible realities.

Together, let us embark on this remarkable journey of impact, and let us leave an indelible mark on the world.

The journey begins *now*.

May L. Harris, June 20, 2023

"It's impossible," said pride.

"It's risky," said experience.

"It's pointless," said reason.

"Give it a try," whispered the heart.

Section 1 | Starting the Journey

> *"No matter what your mission is, have some notion in your head. Forget the model, whether it's government or nonprofit or profit. Ask yourself the more important question: Is my mission improving the world?"*
> - Jeff Bezos
> Founder & Former CEO of Amazon

As an attorney who has specialized in the representation of nonprofit organizations for over two decades, I have had the privilege of working with countless individuals across the country who had the desire and passion to establish a new nonprofit organization. I have spoken with hundreds of founders, who have started all types of charities including animal rescue organizations, preschools, museums, social service institutions, religious organizations and humanitarian relief nonprofits.

Throughout the years, I have found that the most successful nonprofit founders share three primary personality traits.

First, they possess the unique ability of "preception." Etymologically speaking, preception means "to perceive something before it becomes visible."

2

Specifically, it's the ability to see what others cannot, yet. Thus, they can envision the what they must do to improve the world around them.

Second, they possess the ability to craft their vision and articulate their purpose in a way that inspires others to embrace their cause. They are good communicators, and they have the discipline to map out exactly how they are going to achieve their goals.

Finally, successful nonprofit founders leverage what they know to build this new endeavor, and they find consultants, professionals, or other resources to advise them in areas where they are not well-versed. This ability to find and engage others who have knowledge and the expertise they lack, speeds up their journey, and amplifies their overall chances of success.

This book refines and clarifies these three traits, empowering new nonprofit leaders to chart their course to overall success.

Chapter 1 | Envision Change

> "We but mirror the world.
> ... As a man changes his own nature, so does
> the attitude of the world change towards him.
> This is the divine mystery supreme.
> A wonderful thing it is and the source of our
> happiness. We need not wait to see what others
> do."
> – Mahatma Gandhi

Visionaries Demonstrate Preception

The most successful nonprofit founders are those rare individuals who have utilized the trait of preception to recognize an unmet need in their community; they've noticed a gap in available services or resources available to solve a societal problem, and they are driven to make a change.

Jordan Verdin is one of these thought-leaders. His work began when he started documenting the stories of individuals experiencing homelessness in San Diego, California, a location that has struggled over the past decade to adequately address an ever-increasing homeless population. While focusing on these stories, it quickly became clear to him that there were two critical needs that were not currently being met by

4

existing nonprofit organizations or government-run social service agencies: "*the need to be seen and the need to be clean.*"

Verdin observed that lack of access to consistent personal hygiene resources was a major barrier for people experiencing homelessness. He noted that it's practically impossible to obtain a job when you show up to an interview in dirty clothes, with unkempt hair, and - to be frank - you don't smell all that good. Most employers are unlikely to even pay attention to what you have to say, let alone hire you.

He decided that by coordinating mobile showers to be made available where the homeless congregate he could help address that need, as well as providing a sense of dignity to those who may feel marginalized by a system that has failed them.

The nonprofit organization that Verdin founded, Humanity Showers, has grown tremendously since its inception in 2014. The organization currently provides over 2,000 showers per month across three counties in California. Verdin's vision is not just to provide hygiene facilities, but to build bridges between communities and promote greater understanding and compassion for those experiencing homelessness. By sharing the stories and experiences of individuals experiencing homelessness, Verdin and Humanity Showers aim to challenge the stigma and stereotypes of homelessness and empower those who are too often overlooked.

Verdin was able to see what others could not. He noticed a massive gap in available resources and services for those experiencing homelessness, and rather than leaving the issue as one for existing nonprofits or the government to solve, he took action to create a solution.

Visionaries Establish Both Purpose and Vision

At the heart of every successful nonprofit founder is a clear sense of purpose, and an ability to craft a vision of success that appeals to other people. Successful founders must develop a deep understanding of the issues they are trying to address, as well as the discipline to develop a clear vision for what they aim to achieve. This is a key element of their success, as they must be able to articulate the goals and objectives of this new endeavor in a way that inspires others to get involved and support their cause.

Nancy Brinker lost her sister, Susan, to breast cancer when both were young women. That experience led to a driving purpose: she wanted to end the scourge of breast cancer forever, so that no other family would have to experience the loss of a beloved sister, mother, close family member or friend.

So, in 1982 at the age of 36, Brinker founded the Susan G. Komen Breast Cancer Foundation, in honor of her sister.

When Komen was established, breast cancer simply was not discussed. In the 1980s, the topic was practically taboo. Moreover, there was a general lack of education or resources available to those affected by the disease. Fast forward to today, and the foundation has raised and invested over $1 billion in breast cancer research, and more than $2 billion in patient outreach.

Komen's annual Race for the Cure, first conducted in 1983 shortly after the formation of the organization, is one of the most well recognized nonprofit fundraising events in the world. This expansive event takes place in more than 120 U.S. cities and 13 countries. Each year, over 1.5 million people participate in the race, demonstrating their support for those affected by breast cancer and raising critical funds for research and treatment.

The success of the Susan G. Komen Foundation can be attributed to a variety of factors, not the least of which includes Brinker's personal experiences that framed her preception and her purpose. Brinker was able to hone her story, and with dedication, passion and by building a cohesive group of initial stakeholders, she was able to craft and implement her vision.

Visionaries Identify the Challenges

Unfortunately, not all nonprofit organizations are ultimately successful. In fact, many fail within their first few years of operation.

I believe many of these failures are largely due to founders being so intensely passionate about their cause that they rush through the process, fail to take the time to identify the challenges of starting a nonprofit from scratch, and they neglect to search out and find individuals with the knowledge and resources they need to succeed.

In my experience, this haste leads to failure.

Poor Planning

Starting a nonprofit organization requires careful planning. It's important to have a clear understanding of the legal and financial requirements, as well as a strategic plan for how the organization will achieve its goals. Unfortunately, many nonprofit founders fail to strategically map out their mission, vision, goals and objectives and they end up facing significant challenges that many simply cannot overcome.

Nonprofit organizations might not be owned by shareholders who are expecting a return on their investment, but they are "businesses" all the same. Thus, while it might feel odd to say that a nonprofit organization needs a "business" plan, every nonprofit organization needs some type of a plan to map out a path to success.

To differentiate from a traditional "business plan," then, let's use the term *"Strategic Plan,"* instead.

A Strategic Plan is a crucial roadmap for any organization, that outlines the organization's goals, strategies, operational and financial plans, and provides a clear framework for achieving long-term sustainability and success. Without a Strategic Plan, an organization risks becoming directionless, struggling to identify priorities and allocate resources effectively.

A Strategic Plan will also help in the clarification and identification of the organization's brand and messaging, ensuring that the mission and impact of the organization is communicated clearly to stakeholders and to the broader community that they serve. This is a critical element when fundraising, or seeking donor engagement, as donors are more likely to support nonprofits that have a clear and compelling message and a strong plan for achieving their goals.

Despite the critical role that Strategic Plans play in the longevity of nonprofits, many organizations fail to create them or use generic templates that don't reflect their unique needs and goals. This is often due to the perception that planning and strategy development take too much time, and divert resources away from the organization's core mission.

However, the reality is that investing time and resources in developing a comprehensive Strategic Plan is a crucial investment in the long-term sustainability of the organization, and thus its survival. A well-designed plan can help nonprofits identify their strengths, weaknesses, potential challenges, opportunities and threats, enabling them to make informed decisions and adapt to changes in their environment. It can also help them secure funding and build partnerships by demonstrating their commitment to professionalism, transparency, and accountability.

I get it. You want to jump right in and start filling that gap that you've identified, and help as many people as possible as quickly as possible. But you cannot adequately serve others unless you have the foundation in place to support that weight.

No, or Poor, Advice

Many nonprofit founders, faced at the outset with a lack of funds, seek to economize from the start by either doing the bulk of the set up themselves, or hiring "cheap," "inexpensive" or "economy" services to complete the requisite tasks. This is, to use a common British idiom, "penny wise and pound foolish."

In my experience, this early penny-pinching can lead to critical questions not being asked, and important tasks not being done properly, or at all, causing significant cost and delay down the road in order to fix the errors.

LegalZoom is one of many popular online legal service websites that offers low-cost solutions to people who want to avoid paying traditional legal or other professional fees. Unfortunately, LegalZoom, like many other low-cost services, is a "one-size-fits-all" solution, and they provide very little in the way of operational guidance or education. We've already established that you've observed an unmet need, and in most cases have an innovative idea on how to address that need. Innovation and LegalZoom really aren't ideal partners because LegalZoom does not provide personalized advice, and those individuals who use the service often find themselves with generic documents that are not tailored to their specific needs and goals. This can lead to serious problems down the line, as the documents may not be legally valid, meet statutory requirements for tax-exempt status, or align with the requirements of the organization's governing documents.

Nonprofit organizations that are founded on generic documents, incomplete research and templates found online, or ones that demonstrate a lack of planning are likely to struggle with team development, fundraising, program structure, and organizational growth. This can lead to a cycle of financial instability, which ultimately results in the failure of the organization.

Lack of Sustained Financial Support

Like any other organization or business, nonprofit organizations need money to survive. Unlike "for profit" businesses, however, nonprofit organizations cannot generate capital investment by offering equity, and they often aren't thought of as good candidates for lending by banks and other financial institutions.

Without consistent financial support, nonprofit organizations struggle to operate, cannot achieve their mission, and they ultimately fail. This can be due to relying too heavily on a single funding source, struggling to attract and retain donors, failing to effectively manage their finances, or facing unexpected financial challenges.

Ultimately, the key to avoiding failure due to lack of sustained financial support is to focus on building a strong financial foundation. This includes developing a diversified funding base, investing in fundraising and donor retention strategies, and ensuring that the organization has the financial expertise needed to effectively manage its resources.

A successful launch requires planning and expertise.

Chapter 2 | Identify the Path

"Ideas are easy. Implementation is hard."
-Guy Kawasaki, AllTop Co-founder

Starting any new nonprofit venture is a complex process that can be overwhelming, bureaucratic, and full of traps for the unwary.

To successfully navigate the process, it is important to understand that you must wend your way through the intricacies of several state and federal agencies. These agencies are the ones that oversee formations of new legal entities on the state level, the granting or denial of federal and state-level tax-exempt status, and state-level registration to solicit and hold charitable funds. This last step is one that is often overlooked by many of the inexpensive online options available to founders, as well as many CPAs (as registration is a legal requirement, not a tax or financial requirement).

Pitfalls and traps for the unwary founder are littered throughout the formation process.

Forming a Separate Entity

The first legal step in forming a nonprofit organization involves creating a legal entity that is recognized by the state in which you are located or wish to operate. This process typically involves drafting and filing articles of incorporation with the appropriate state agency, which creates a new, separate legal entity that can enter into contracts, own property, and conduct business separate from its founders.

Many states have "form" articles of incorporation, that are simply fill-in-the-blank PDF documents. It's tempting to use these forms for ease of use, and it would seem that if the division of corporations or Secretary of State created it, the form would contain all the provisions required of a nonprofit, tax-exempt organization as it begins i's lifecycle, and as it grows.

Unfortunately, this is not always the case.

Several of our firm's clients came to us midway through their formation and exemption process. They had attempted to complete the maze of paperwork themselves, but had to resort to seeking legal counsel when it became too overwhelming for them to complete, or they had received a denial of exemption.

In a few cases, these clients had utilized the form articles of incorporation provided by the California Secretary of State, and all thought they had completed the form correctly. At that time, however, there was a "check the box" question related to the specific purpose of the new organization which had the options of "charitable," "public" or "charitable and public." These clients had selected only "public." As we work often with IRS exempt-organizations examiners, those hardy individuals tasked with reviewing tens of thousands of exemption applications every year, we knew that some examiners took the view that "public" was not an exempt purpose under the 501(c)(3) statute, and at least in one situation we were familiar with, had initially rejected an application due to the "public" box being checked, resulting in the need to amend the articles of incorporation in order to receive tax exempt status.

Thus, even the *very first filing* you are asked to complete to start the process can have traps for the unwary.

Once the articles of incorporation have been filed, then it's time to hold a formal meeting, whereby organizational bylaws are adopted, directors are appointed, officers are elected, and other formal business is discussed and approved.

It's common at this stage for clients to ask me if they can be the sole director of the new organization. While normal business corporations can have only one director, for several reasons including an inherent conflict of interest, it's not in the best interest of nonprofit organizations that are seeking to become a 501(c)(3) tax-exempt organization to do the same.

Typically, our firm recommends that a founder find a minimum of three, unrelated individuals who will agree to serve on a new nonprofit board of directors. Then, those directors can each also serve as the three required officer positions of president, secretary and treasurer.

Further, as previously mentioned, it is often in the best interest of a founder to find supplementary individuals who can provide expertise that a sole founder may not possess.

Finally, to complete the formation of this new corporate entity, you must also obtain a new Federal Employer Identification Number (FEIN or EIN) from the Internal Revenue Service (IRS). Sometimes, we see errors made in the initial filing applying for the FEIN, as the online process for obtaining the FEIN for a nonprofit tax-exempt organization requires selecting a box entitled "other" which is located at the end of a list of options that would ordinarily seem reasonable to select.

Once received, the FEIN serves two functions. The first is to identify the organization as a separate "taxpayer" in the eyes of the IRS. You will be using this number frequently, including when you open a bank account that is tied to the organization, rather than yourself as founder. Second, if you plan to accept charitable gifts, grants, or contributions once you receive tax-exempt status, you need to provide this number to the donor to facilitate their tax reporting as well.

Once you have completed these steps, you are able to operate separately from yourself as a nonprofit organization, even though you are not (yet) tax-exempt.

Qualifying for Exemption from Income Tax

It's important to understand that just because you successfully establish your new corporation as a nonprofit, that doesn't automatically make it tax-exempt.

In order to obtain tax-exempt status, which is critical to most nonprofit organizations, you must successfully apply for and obtain recognition of exemption from the Internal Revenue Service and, in some cases, with a state level taxing agency. To gain tax-exempt status under Section 501(c)(3), you must apply by submitting either the *Form 1023 Application for Recognition of Exemption*, or the shorter (and cheaper) *Form 1023-EZ Short Form Application for Recognition of Exemption*, to the IRS.[1]

Fundamentally, nonprofit organizations that have been granted exempt status under Section 501(c)(3) must meet two tests; the "Organizational" test and the "Operational" test. Further, the organization cannot be overly "commercial" in nature.

The Organizational Test

To pass the Organizational Test, a nonprofit organization must be obligated to dedicate its assets to exempt purposes (religious, charitable, educational,

---

[1] Other nonprofit organizations that serve other non-charitable community purposes, such as social welfare organizations exempt under Section 501(c)(4), or business leagues or chambers of commerce exempt under Section 501(c)(6), will instead utilize the Form 1024 application for exemption.

literary, etc.) in perpetuity, either pursuant to its governing documents or applicable state law. This means that, in addition to being required to apply its assets for exclusively exempt purposes throughout its lifecycle, an organization is also required to dedicate any remaining assets for those exempt purposes if the organization ever dissolves.

An organization would fail the Organizational Test if, for example, it was permitted to distribute dividends to shareholders, a for-profit company, or if it was empowered to distribute remaining assets to its members on dissolution.

The Operational Test

The Operational Test evaluates how the nonprofit organization actually operates. In other words, it is an evaluation of whether an organization's activities correspond to the organizational requirements. To pass the Operational Test, an organization cannot

- Engage in more than insubstantial noncharitable activity (including commercial activity or lobbying activities);
- Engage in any prohibited political campaign activity;

◻   Distribute its net earnings "in whole or in part to the benefit of private shareholders or individuals" (also known as "private inurement")

Even any "insubstantial" commercial activity gives rise to "unrelated business income," which is revenue generated from activities unrelated to the organization's exempt purpose. This type of revenue should be limited to protect the exempt status of the organization, and the net income from that activity reported to the IRS using Form 990-T.

Private Inurement

Finally, no part of the organization's net earnings may "inure to the benefit of" shareholders or individuals, except through reasonable compensation for services rendered or fair market value transactions. If these transactions are not reasonable, they are considered "excess benefit" transactions. Over time, this concept has been distilled into the "Private Inurement" and "Private Benefit" principles.

"Private Inurement" refers to the use of an organization's activities, income or assets for the personal benefit of individuals with a close relationship to the organization.

"Private Benefit" is quite a bit broader than Private Inurement and the concept includes individuals and businesses that do not have a close relationship with the nonprofit organization. Private Benefit includes individuals or businesses that receive an unfair advantage from an organization's services.

Intermediate Sanctions

Violation of the Private Inurement restrictions can lead to pretty severe consequences.

It used to be that if Private Inurement occurred, the IRS would quickly revoke the exempt status of the organization. In 1996, however, the IRS instituted an "intermediate" remedy, rather than full revocation of tax-exempt status. Codified in Section 4958 of the Internal Revenue Code, these sanctions allow the IRS to impose "excise taxes" on the excess benefit transaction between a disqualified person (an insider) and the nonprofit. The excise taxes are assessed against the disqualified person that benefited from the transaction, as well as any officer, director or organizational manager who approved the transaction.

So how much of a tax are we talking about?

Well, it's equal to 25 percent of the value of the excess benefit. If the 25 percent tax is imposed, and the excess benefit transaction is not corrected within the relevant tax period, an additional excise tax of 200 percent of the excess benefit will be imposed.

In other words, it's nothing to sneeze at.

Applying for Recognition of Tax-Exempt Status

Once you have made sure that your organization will pass the Organizational Test, the Operational Test, and you have put in place controls to ensure that you won't be overly benefiting an individual or business, you're ready to apply for "tax-exempt" status. After all, this preferential tax treatment means that your nonprofit organization will not have to pay federal income tax on the funds you receive. Further, if you have been recognized as exempt under Section 501(c)(3), then it also means that your donors can deduct their contributions to you from their personal income taxes, which can be a big incentive for them to support your organization.

The IRS estimates that completing the full Form 1023 application will take about fourteen (14) hours for an average person to truly understand, and complete. The IRS instructions for the form are 40 pages in length, comprising three columns of fine print, with detailed instructions regarding each and every line of the application. Depending upon your organization's complexity and the need for additional schedules, drafting responses to the IRS's questions can be quite time-consuming, as you need to provide detailed information about your organization's activities, finances, and governance.

Further, once submitted, the application itself can take six months to wend its way through the IRS on its way to being evaluated by an examiner.

One of the reasons the application is so complex, is that the IRS wants to make sure that only organizations that meet the statutory criteria obtain tax-exempt status. Specifically, as we discussed earlier, in order to receive exemption under Section 501(c)(3), the organization must meet the Organizational and Operational tests, and be organized and operated for exempt purposes, which include religious, charitable, educational, literary, and/or scientific purposes.

Also, you'll recall the prohibition against private inurement, and the application for exemption is drafted in such a way that it teases out any potential impermissible benefit, and you are asked to demonstrate that if your organization receives exemption, you will not be promoting your own personal gain.

Many online services offer to complete your exemption application, and it's tempting to choose a company that promises you a determination of exemption in only a few weeks, while charging very low fees. What these companies typically do, however, is utilize the shorter, easier version of the Form 1023 application, the 1023-EZ, even if you don't really qualify. This version, while shorter, easier, and less-expensive than its more complex sibling, is meant for very small organizations that can attest, under penalty of perjury, that they estimate they will raise less than $50,000 in gross receipts for each of the first three years of their existence.

Further, many self-preparers will use the 1023-EZ application without really understanding the restrictions. The IRS asks that 1023-EZ applicants complete a worksheet confirming their eligibility prior to submitting an application, ensuring the new organization has completed all the steps required for tax-exemption.

In my experience, however, many founders simply do not complete this step. We had a client at FPLG who had received tax exempt status utilizing the 1023-EZ, but hadn't completed formation on the state level, first. They just didn't understand the process.

We often are asked if there is a way to convert the application from a 1023-EZ to a full 1023 in the future, if they realize there has been an error, or they did something incorrectly. Unfortunately, the answer to that question is "no." You get one shot at successfully applying for exempt status, and any future information that comes to light would need to be shared with the IRS using the organization's annual informational tax filings.

Additionally, a common error made by both novice applicants as well as a few of the popular online services is checking a single box incorrectly on either the full 1023 application, or on the 1023-EZ. This single error can result in a misclassification of a new organization as a private foundation, rather than as a public charity.

Under the tax code, there are two primary types of organizations that qualify for exempt status under Section 501(c)(3): **private foundations** and **public**

charities. Thus, you might ask, "does it really matter, then? We would still have 501(c)(3) status..."

Well, yes. It does matter.

Private foundations are typically established by high-net-worth individuals, families, or businesses with the primary purpose of providing financial grants to deserving public charities. There are variances, but private foundations typically do not operate programs outside of their grant making and general community support.

The annual tax filings for private foundations, the 990-PF, is much more complex than the regular tax filings for exempt organizations, primarily because organizations characterized as a private foundation are subject to a host of regulations that public charities are not, including payment of an excise tax on investment income and rules pertaining to excess business holdings.

Public charities, on the other hand, are expected to garner financial support from the general public, not an individual or small group of donors. Thus, the IRS requires charities to meet something called the "public support test." A nonprofit public charity must receive

33.33% or more of its total support from donors (or individuals paying for the services of the nonprofit) who give less than 2% of the organization's overall receipts in order to maintain its classification as a public charity.

In rare cases, this misclassification may be caught by an eagle-eyed IRS examiner if the applicant has prepared a well-crafted full 1023 application, with a descriptive narrative of activities. However, because the Form 1023-EZ applications are **not reviewed by an IRS agent**, nor do they require a robust description of the nonprofit's activities and charitable purpose, if that one box is incorrectly checked on the 1023-EZ, the organization will be incorrectly classified as a private foundation. To rectify the error, an applicant then must complete yet another IRS application, a Request for Miscellaneous Determination, pay an additional user fee (which is currently twice the amount of the original application fee), and wait several more months to be properly re-classified in the IRS Master File.

Charitable Solicitation Registration

Most states have laws that require charitable organizations to register with a state agency before they can solicit donations from the public. These laws are based on a set of guidelines called the Charleston Principles, which were developed by state charity officials to promote transparency and accountability in charitable fundraising, and to help ensure the funds raised were expended on charitable or educational purposes.

States who have adopted provisions similar to the Charleston Principles require charities to provide information about their fundraising activities, including how much money they raise and how the money is spent. By registering, charities are providing this information to charity regulators and ensuring that they are being held accountable for their fundraising activities.

The consequences of not registering to fundraise can be severe. Charities that fail to register can face fines and penalties (which often cannot be paid by the organization, but must be paid by the individual directors), and may even be forced to cease their fundraising activities. Additionally, failing to register can make it more difficult to attract donors.

In some cases, failing to register can also result in legal action by state charity officials or the attorney general. These legal actions can be costly and time-consuming, result in loss of your organization's tax-exempt status, and can have a lasting impact on a charity's ability to operate.

Fundraising in More Than One State

As your organization grows, you might find that your fundraising or solicitation activities cross state lines. Indeed, if you solicit financial support on your website, some states take the view that you are fundraising in that state, and you have a registration requirement.

If you plan to fundraise in multiple states, it's important to know that you will need to comply with *each state's* charitable solicitation registration requirements. This can be a complex and time-consuming process, as each state has its own registration requirements, fees, deadlines, and processes for renewal and reporting.

One option for charities that fundraise in multiple states is to start by using the unified registration statement sponsored by the National Association of State Charity Officials (NASCO). While not approved and in-use in all states that require registration, this unified statement allows charities to register with several states through a single application. This can save some time and simplify the registration process for charities that fundraise in those states.

It's important to note that even if the NASCO registration is used, you may still be required to file additional paperwork or meet other requirements in the NASCO states, or to submit individual registrations in non-NASCO states. It's important to understand the requirements for each state and to ensure that you are in compliance with all applicable laws and regulations.

Chapter 3 | Understand the Structure

"Any fool can know. The point is to understand."
— Albert Einstein

Serving on the board of a nonprofit organization can be one of the most fulfilling roles you will ever experience. However, it does also bring an increase in overall responsibility and, in some cases, personal liability and risk.

Fiduciary Duties

As a board member, you owe various *fiduciary duties* to the organization.

The concept of a fiduciary duty has existed for thousands of years and has been central to the development of functional civilizations. Indeed, academics point to Hammurabi's Code, which was developed around 1790 BCE, as including a fiduciary relationship when discussing the rules of agency. Further, Confucius wrote in *The Analects*, a heuristic for fiduciaries, "In acting on behalf of others, have I always been loyal to their interest?"

Finally, the Romans actually coined the term "fiduciary," and defined it as "a person holding the character of a trustee, or a character analogous of a trustee, in respect to the trust and confidence involved in it and the scrupulous good faith and candor which it requires."

In the simplest terms, a fiduciary duty arises when one person relies on another to perform a task or service. Over the last hundred years or so of jurisprudence, the primary fiduciary duties owed by a director to their organization have evolved to include the duty of care, the duty of inquiry, the duty of loyalty, and the duty of obedience.

The Duty of Care

Specifically, the duty of care requires each board member to exercise *reasonable care* in overseeing the affairs of the organization, including making informed decisions and overseeing the management of that organization. At minimum, this means directors are required to actively participate in board meetings, work to advance the mission and vision of the organization, monitor the financial health of the organization, and engage in strategic planning to ensure the long-term health of the organization.

The Duty of Inquiry

Sometimes combined with the Duty of Care, but not always, is the Duty of Inquiry. Directors of nonprofit organizations must pay attention to and monitor the activities of the organization, and if they notice anything suspicious or out of the ordinary, they are required to do whatever is reasonably required to inform themselves, and determine the cause. In fulfilling this duty, directors may rely upon guidance provided by reliable and competent persons on matters which the director believes to be within such person's professional or expert competence. This can include accountants, attorneys, and other professionals.

The Duty of Loyalty

The duty of loyalty requires board members to act in the best interest of the organization, and not in their own best interest, those of their family members, or any other individual or for-profit business. Further, directors must promptly disclose any potential conflicts of interest, and allow other, disinterested members of the board determine the path forward.

The Duty of Obedience

Finally, the duty of obedience requires board members to ensure that the organization follows its governing documents, and that it complies with all legal and statutory requirements. The directors must remain "obedient" to the mission and stated purposes of the organization and should not authorize or allow the organization to pursue unrelated or improper activities.

Additional Fiduciary Duties

In addition, over time a few additional duties have been applied to officers and directors of nonprofit organizations by both statute and through various court rulings. For example, the duty of prudence requires board members to make investment decisions that are in the best interests of the organization, and the duty of confidentiality requires board members to keep sensitive information confidential.

Accounting for Charitable Assets

As a nonprofit organization, the challenge of adequately accounting for the funds received and the expenses made can be a daunting task. Many people do not understand that there are several primary differences between how nonprofit organizations and businesses account for their revenue and expenses.

Like their "for-profit" counterparts, nonprofit accounting is governed by generally accepted accounting principles (GAAP), but it has some unique features.

First, nonprofits don't have equity; they have net assets, which are typically divided into three separate funds: unrestricted, temporarily restricted, and permanently restricted. This makes sense, when you think about it, as nonprofit tax-exempt organizations do not have shareholders who can hold "equity," so they do not need to distribute earnings, but they do need to track how funds are obtained and any restrictions on how they are to be spent.

In nonprofit accounting, each type of fund has its own set of accounting rules:

- *Restricted funds.* These are the funds that must be spent on certain projects and activities at your organization, and are often a condition of accepting grants or gifts from donors or private foundations;
- **Temporarily restricted funds**. These funds must be spent on certain projects and activities of the nonprofit until the expiration of a certain time period. After that time, they can be moved to unrestricted funds;

□ **Unrestricted funds.** All funds in this category can be spent on whatever goals, initiatives, or general expenses of the nonprofit require the greatest need.

Obviously, nonprofit organizations typically try to maximize the amount of unrestricted funds they receive from supporters, as that provides them the freedom to spend the funds however they see fit.

In the end, nonprofit accounting focuses on both transparency and accountability. Donors and charity regulators want to know that the contributions you have been given are being used appropriately, and this requires careful record-keeping. In addition to keeping track of all funds received and spent, including any restrictions or conditions placed on them by donors, nonprofits must also prepare detailed financial statements (not just bank statements).

Finally, at the heart of any accounting system is a "chart of accounts." A chart of accounts for a nonprofit organization differs fundamentally from a business chart of accounts as the nonprofit must track those restricted and unrestricted funds separately, and then each fund should have unique revenue and expense sub-accounts. For example, funds that are restricted for a particular purpose should separately track the funds received, the expenses incurred on that particular purpose, and the balance left in the fund.

Finally, in many states nonprofits are required to obtain an independent audit of their financial statements, typically when receipts exceed a certain monetary threshold, which varies state by state. Thus, in many states a nonprofit organization must establish an audit committee, separate from the finance committee, to ensure that financial statements are accurate, and that the organization is compliant with GAAP and IRS regulations. In those states without a statutory requirement to have such a committee, it's still best practice to do so.

Accounting for nonprofits can be time-consuming and requires specialized expertise. While an organization is young it may not have the resources to hire a full-time accountant or to invest in the necessary software and training, thus, outsourcing of your accounting services can be a practical solution.

Finally, it's critically important for nonprofit organizations to put in place a financial policies and procedures manual, to set sound financial guidelines for the nonprofit that promote prudent fiscal management, to abide by Generally Accepted Accounting Principles (GAAP), and to ensure ongoing legal compliance.

At minimum, this manual should include policies and procedures addressing

- Monthly, quarterly, and annual accounting procedures;
- Internal financial controls;
- Financial Planning & Reporting;
- Revenue/Accounts Receivable;
- Expense/Accounts Payable; and
- Asset Management.

A robust accounting manual will serve to protect the assets of the organization, ensuring that the organization maintains accurate and timely records of the nonprofit's financial activities, provide a framework for programmatic decision making and staff training, and ensure ongoing compliance with federal, state, and local legal and reporting requirements.

Risks of Poor Governance

Attention of Charity Regulators

Nonprofit organizations often hold charitable assets, such as property, endowments, and funds contributed by members of the community. With the acceptance of these charitable assets, comes the responsibility to manage them in the best interests of the organization and the public.

Nonprofit directors have the duty to ensure that the funds they hold on behalf of the public are used for their intended purposes. If they do not, they run the risk of becoming an audit target of their state attorney general as well as the Internal Revenue Service.

In most states, the attorney general has the authority to investigate and take legal action against nonprofits that fail to comply with state laws governing charitable assets. This oversight is designed to protect the public's interest in ensuring that charitable assets are used for their intended purposes and that nonprofit organizations are fulfilling their fiduciary duties.

The attorney general can focus their attention upon your nonprofit organization due to inconsistencies in your annual reports and filings, or because some member of the public has submitted a complaint or report of improper activities against you. Typically, as soon as the attorney general believes that there has been wrongdoing, they proceed to request a great deal of information, both financial statements and all corporate records, including meeting minutes (keep well-organized records of these). Thereafter, if they feel further action is warranted, they can file suit against the organization, its officers and its directors.

Member Derivative Lawsuits

Some nonprofit organizations are either required to have statutory members, or they have chosen to include provisions allowing for a sense of democracy within their organization. In that case, members may have the right to elect directors, have a say in distribution of the organization's assets, or the right to authorize any significant corporate changes such as bylaw revision, or dissolution.

Sometimes, a member might believe that in order to adequately protect their perceived rights, ensure a nonprofit organization follows the law, or because they believe that a director has breached their fiduciary duties, they choose to file a lawsuit to protect and enforce their rights.

These lawsuits seek to hold the board members accountable for their actions, and they can not only be incredibly complex to litigate, they can also be extremely expensive to defend.

Chapter 4 | Navigate the Financials

"The world does not lack the financial resources to feed,
educate and clothe its inhabitants.
Rather, it lacks leaders committed to addressing
the problems of the impoverished."
— Óscar Arias

As a nonprofit founder or board member, one of your biggest challenges will always be raising money to support your organization's mission and programs. With so many organizations and individuals competing for donor dollars, it can feel overwhelming and incredibly discouraging at times.

One of the most important things to keep in mind is that donors want to feel like they are making a real impact. They want to know that their money is going towards something meaningful, and that it will make a tangible difference in the world. This means that you need to be able to clearly communicate your organization's mission, goals, and accomplishments to potential donors.

When approaching donors, it's important to be strategic. Many organizations just send out a mass email or generic fundraising letter and then hope for the best. Instead, successful nonprofits take the time to research potential donors, and tailor their approach to match the donor's interests and values.

Another important factor in convincing people to give to a nonprofit organization is authenticity and transparency. Donors want to know that their money is being used responsibly, and that the organization they have chosen to support is both accountable and responsive. This means a successful nonprofit is open about its financials, provides regular updates on the impact its activities and programs are making, and demonstrates a commitment to good governance and ethical practices.

Finally, many nonprofits forget about the power of storytelling. People are more likely to give when they can connect emotionally with the cause they are supporting. Sharing personal stories of how an organization has made a difference in the lives of people, animals or upon the environment can be a powerful way to engage potential donors and inspire them to give.

Ultimately, raising money for a nonprofit may always be a challenge. But by focusing on communicating impact, being strategic in how donors are approached, demonstrating transparency, and telling compelling stories, any nonprofit can increase its chances of success and make a real difference in the world.

It is a common misconception that a nonprofit must spend all the money it brings in each year; perhaps it is from the use of the word "nonprofit," assuming that there can be no "profit." This is simply not the case. While the purpose of a nonprofit is not to generate profit for shareholders or owners, but rather to serve the organization's mission and its beneficiaries, this doesn't mean that a nonprofit can't accumulate funds and carry them over from one year to the next.

In fact, having a healthy reserve of funds can be crucial to the long-term sustainability of any nonprofit organization. It allows the organization to weather unexpected expenses, downturns in revenue, or changes in the overall economy. Funders and donors also want to see that their contributions are being used effectively, and that the organization has a sound financial footing which can be affected if insufficient reserves are held.

Earned Revenue or Fee-For-Service

Often in our legal practice, we get asked whether a nonprofit can charge for the services they provide.

After all, if a nonprofit charges for its service, then doesn't that mean it's making a profit just like a business? This is a common misconception, and the answer is actually, "no."

Think about it. Most of us have visited museums, enrolled our children in summer camps offered by the YMCA, or paid an "adoption fee" when bringing home a pet from the local animal shelter. These are all examples of nonprofit organizations who are charging fees, albeit likely reduced fees, to the public to take advantage of the services they provide.

Where nonprofit organizations get into trouble, however, is when their earned revenue is made as a result of commercial business activity that is not related to their purpose.

Unrelated Business Activity

As mentioned previously, nonprofit organizations are exempt from paying taxes on most of their revenue streams, but this exemption does not apply to all forms of income. The Unrelated Business Income Tax (UBIT) is a federal tax on the income that is **not related to the organization's exempt purpose**. This tax is levied on the gross income, minus the expenses directly connected to that income. In other words, if a nonprofit earns revenue from an activity unrelated to its mission, it may be subject to income tax.

For instance, a nonprofit might decide to raise funds by renting out an unused parking lot, selling apparel, or by offering advertising space in their newsletter. This activity may generate much needed revenue, but as these types of activities are typically not related to the nonprofit's exempt purpose, the income generated from these activities is likely to be subject to UBIT, and must be disclosed and paid with the filing of the Form 990-T.

While these strategies might be useful in raising some extra funds, it's important to keep in mind that not only might the revenue be taxable, but you might also need to collect and remit sales tax for the sale of merchandise in most states. Further, if these unrelated activities get to be too great, it can put the tax-exempt status of the organization at risk as the Internal Revenue Service will take the position that the organization is too "commercial" in nature, and not truly organized and operated for exempt purposes.

Third-Party Fundraisers

If you have school aged children, you've experienced at least one form of a third-party fundraiser. The most common of these "commercial co-venture" events come in the form of a restaurant night or other business donating a percentage of their daily sales they receive from a particular nonprofit's supporters.

It's easy to see why many organizations believe these types of fundraisers are a good idea; but they might, in reality, be lost opportunities where it might have been a better idea to do something different.

For example, let's say that your organization is offered 5% of the proceeds at your local restaurant from everyone who mentions your nonprofit organization during one evening, between the hours of 5 and 7pm. You advertise the restaurant night on Facebook, Twitter, and in your newsletter.

One of your supporters, who typically donates around $100 to your organization, sees the deal and brings her husband, two kids, and grandparents to this restaurant for dinner just to support the sponsoring nonprofit organization. They wrap up the evening with a $200 bill. The supporter feels great about spending money at this restaurant even while acknowledging that she would have spent much less than $200 on a home cooked meal. As a result, she feels like she has done her part to support the organization, and she ignores the solicitations she receives the rest of the year.

As a result of the event, the restaurant contributes $10 to you, representing 5% of the check. But your supporter forgoes her normal $100 donation because she spent $200 at the restaurant night. At the end of the day, your organization actually lost about $90 or so - from just this one supporter.

Fundraising Platforms

The next most common fundraising ideas includes the use of third-party fundraising platforms, or ancillary funding such as the now-wound down Amazon Smile or the ubiquitous GoFundMe. While these platforms- and others - offer excellent tools to raise some money, they're not all that sustainable. While these platforms provide an opportunity to raise a little money, they also have some limitations.

Amazon Smile, for instance, up until February of 2023 would donate a very small percentage of the price of eligible purchases to the charitable organization of the customer's choice. While this may have seemed like a great opportunity, most nonprofit organizations found it difficult to be able to harness enough supporters buying on your behalf to support any real programming. Similarly, while GoFundMe campaigns can help raise money quickly, they may not be a long-term solution to sustain the organization's operations and the platform takes quite a large "chunk" of the funds in fees.

Creative (But Sometimes Risky) Ways Nonprofits Raise Funds

Raffles, Bingo, and other "Games of Chance"

Holding raffles, bingo games, and other games of chance seems like an easy and fun way to raise money, and sometimes these games can be rather lucrative. However, there are significant challenges and regulations that nonprofits must consider before hosting that charity poker or bingo night.

First and foremost, nonprofits must ensure that the state in which they are located allows these types of games. Each state has different laws and regulations that govern gambling and games of chance, and failure to follow those regulations can actually be considered a crime in many states, leading to criminal prosecution.

Raising Funds through Vehicle Donation

We've all seen the commercials, and we've all heard the jingle. Raising funds through vehicle donation is a popular fundraising method, and "Cars for Kids" might be the most recognizable to the general public. Due to the potential for fraud and abuse, however, this particular fundraising mechanism has been the subject of increased scrutiny among charity regulators at both the federal and state levels for many years.

One of the biggest issues with starting a vehicle donation program is ensuring the nonprofit's messaging doesn't give the impression donors can use inflated valuations for their vehicles because they are giving it to charity. Nonprofit organizations have been audited by the IRS for implying that donors could take a deduction equal to the "blue book" value, regardless of the condition of the vehicle, or whether it was even operational.

At the end of the day, nonprofit organizations need to diversify their revenue streams to support their programs and activities. While alternative revenue streams like selling products or services, renting out facilities or ad spaces may provide additional funding, they may also create tax liabilities that must be factored into the decision. As a nonprofit, it is crucial to understand the tax implications of these activities to determine the best way to generate income that aligns with your mission while avoiding any unwanted tax liabilities.

Chapter 5 | Evaluate the Risk

"We'll try to cooperate fully with the IRS, because, as citizens, we feel a strong patriotic duty not to go to jail."
— Dave Barry

The risk of personal criminal or civil liability on the part of individual nonprofit board members is small, but it does exist.

Board members don't have to be perfect in their decision making to avoid personal liability; they can make bad decisions, or they could rely on poorly chosen "experts" whose advice is later determined to be erroneous without resulting in personal liability on the part of individual board members. This means that board members who act in "good faith" and with reasonable diligence and ordinary care, are unlikely to be held personally liable for their actions on the part of the nonprofit organization.

There are, however, a number of specific situations that create or increase the exposure to personal liability.

Breach of Fiduciary Duty

As discussed in Chapter 3, directors of nonprofit organizations serve in a fiduciary capacity to that organization, and sometimes "breach" those duties, even accidentally. Because the duties are owed to the organization, the director can face claims brought by their fellow directors, officers of the organization, state attorneys general, statutory members, and the Internal Revenue Service.

When that happens, they can face liability from lawsuits filed by other directors, members, or charity regulators for that breach.

Excess Benefit Transactions

According to the IRS, an excess benefit transaction is any transaction where an economic benefit is provided **by** a tax-exempt organization, directly or indirectly, **to or for the use of** a "disqualified person," and the "value of the economic benefit provided by the organization **exceeds the value** of the consideration received by the organization" (emphasis added).

So, what is a "disqualified person"? Well, again, the IRS defines a disqualified person as "any person who was in a position to exercise substantial influence over the affairs of the applicable tax-exempt organization... It is not necessary that the person actually exercise substantial influence, only that the person be in a position to do so."

In a nutshell, that means any officer, director or high-level manager will likely be considered as being in a position to exercise substantial influence. Further, family members of the disqualified person, as well as the entities controlled by the disqualified person, are also disqualified persons.

Most often, organizations and their directors are found to have violated the excess benefit rules in one of two ways: compensating their managers, and entering into lucrative contracts with disqualified persons or entities.

Here's an example.

Let's say that a board member of a large, environmentally focused nonprofit organization was also the owner of an up-and-coming carbon sequestration company. After all, those two missions would likely be aligned. This board member pitches his company's quite expensive services to the board, and the board does little in the way of exploring "fair market value" for the services that will be provided.

After little discussion, other than the board discussing how great it is that more carbon will be sequestered as a result of their actions, the board agrees to enter into a multi-year, million dollar contract with the board member's company.

This is an excess benefit transaction.

Section 4958 of the Internal Revenue Code imposes a pretty steep excise tax on these types of excess benefit transactions that occur between a disqualified person and the nonprofit organization. The disqualified person who benefits from an excess benefit transaction is liable for the excise tax representing 25% of the excess benefit, and if the excess benefit transaction is not corrected within the taxable period, an additional excise tax equal to 200% of the excess benefit is imposed.

In our example, this type of transaction is likely also a violation of the private inurement prohibition discussed in Chapter 2, leading to personal liability of the board members or managers who approved the contract.

Political Campaign Activity

In 1954, then–Senator Lyndon Johnson sponsored legislation in Congress that would prohibit churches and other nonprofit organizations that are exempt from taxation from directly or indirectly participating in, or intervening in, any political campaign on behalf of, or in opposition to, any candidate for elective public office. In essence, nonprofit organizations could no longer sponsor or support specific politicians or parties. Since passage of what came to be known as the "Johnson Amendment," organizations that have received tax-exempt status are completely prohibited from collecting contributions on behalf of political campaigns, or making any statement for or against a particular candidate for public office.

Certain voter education activities, including presenting public forums and publishing voter education materials, conducted in a non-partisan manner do not constitute prohibited political campaign activity. However, voter education or registration activities with evidence of bias that favors one candidate over another, opposes an individual candidate in some manner, or has the effect of favoring one candidate or group of candidates based on political affiliation, constitutes prohibited participation or intervention.

There are legal methods of engaging in advocacy and legislative activity that we explore in Chapter 7. The consequences of doing it outside of those methods, and violating this prohibition may result in revocation of a nonprofit organization's tax-exempt status, as well as the imposition of an excise tax of 10% of the political expenditure assessed against the organization, plus a 2.5% tax on any manager who approved it.

Further, if the expenditure isn't promptly corrected, those amounts rise to 100% and 50%, respectively.

People Risk

People are what drive the mission and vision of a charitable nonprofit. They are the heartbeat of any organization, and they also pose the greatest risk to that same organization.

Some of this risk can be self-imposed, inadvertently brought upon the organization by naive directors when determining how to classify their workers.

Other liabilities can arise from disgruntled employees who were simply poor hiring choices from the start, or that may have legitimate claims against the nonprofit organization because they have been underpaid, harassed, or discriminated against in some way. Unfortunately, many states have provisions for statutory damages, and statutory attorney's fees, against employers in these situations, and violations of those provisions can be extremely expensive to handle.

Worker Classification

It is a common misconception, prevalent among many small nonprofit organizations, that "employment laws are different for nonprofit organizations." This typically pops up when an organization decides to hire its first employee. Founders sometimes believe that they can freely choose between characterizing that worker as either an independent contractor or as an employee.

With that mistaken understanding, most nonprofit founders will choose to characterize the worker as an independent contractor. Why? Because it's cheaper.

By classifying a worker as an independent contractor, rather than an employee, the nonprofit organization can avoid payment of the employer's share of payroll taxes, including Medicare and Social Security, as well as avoiding unemployment insurance payments that may be required if the worker was classified as an employee.

In other words, an independent contractor is generally considered to be self-employed and is responsible for paying his or her own self-employment taxes, while an employee is subject to withholding taxes and other employment taxes, which the employer is responsible for paying.

Unfortunately, the proper classification of a worker is not an option to choose between based simply upon expense; it is an analysis of responsibilities, job expectations, control, and the overall function of the position. Getting the analysis wrong results in misclassification of that worker, which can result in serious tax consequences for a nonprofit organization.

If a worker is found to have been misclassified as an independent contractor, for example, but should have been classified as an employee, the organization may be held responsible for unpaid taxes, penalties, and interest. They will be required to pay back overdue payroll taxes that should have been withheld from the worker's wages in the first place, including both Social Security and Medicare taxes. These penalties can be significant, ranging from 1.5% to 10% of the total amount of employment taxes owed, depending on the severity of the violation.

Further, the IRS has the authority to hold an organization's officers and directors (those with fiduciary responsibility for the organization) personally responsible for the oversight; the "corporate shield" normally in place between the activities of the organization and the personal pockets of the individuals in charge, simply disappears.

Employment Related Lawsuits

As mentioned previously, nonprofit organizations must adhere to federal and state employment laws, just like their "for-profit" counterparts. These laws govern minimum wage, overtime pay, and other wage-related issues. Again, just like with worker misclassification, failure to comply with these laws can result in lawsuits and costly penalties. Specifically, nonprofit employers must ensure that they keep accurate records of hours worked by each employee, maintain up-to-date personnel files, and provide employees with accurate information regarding their pay.

Often, fledgling nonprofit organizations in a cash crunch will ask their employees to forebear, or wait for their paycheck until the nonprofit can replenish its cash. This is a critical mistake; failing to pay employees on time or correctly can result in statutory penalties and required payment of an employee's legal fees.

Harassment and discrimination in the workplace are also significant risks for nonprofit organizations, especially ones that do not have robust employment manuals or policies, or adequate processes to address complaints in place.

Nonprofit organizations have the responsibility to create a safe and respectful work environment that is free from any form of harassment or discrimination. This requires establishing and implementing policies and procedures that address these issues, training employees on appropriate behavior, and taking swift and appropriate action in response to any allegations of harassment or discrimination.

Employees can also bring suit for something called "wrongful termination." Nonprofit employers must ensure that they document any and all issues with the employee, and follow proper procedures when a decision to terminate employment is made. Failure to do so can result in wrongful termination lawsuits that can be incredibly expensive and time-consuming.

Contract Disputes

It's inevitable that, as your organization grows, you will enter into various contracts for services, supplies or equipment. Some of the first contracts you might enter as a nonprofit might be subscription contracts for the use of software, email, or with vendors to create websites or marketing campaigns.

Whatever the contract may be, for those either inexperienced with various contract provisions, or those who tend not to "read all of the fine print," there are a few primary contract terms that you should make sure are included in any agreements you sign.

The Parties

This might seem overly simple, but you will want to make sure that the contract is between the right entities and individuals. For new organizations, it's critical to have the contract reflect the nonprofit corporation as the party, not the founder as an individual. Further, it's important to check the organization's bylaws to ensure that the individual signing on behalf of the nonprofit has been empowered to do so, and that they have obtained board approval if required.

Purposes of the Agreement

Think about the purpose of the agreement, and why you are entering into a contract in the first place. For example, does the vendor you have selected to build your website have the qualifications necessary to do so? A brief description of the vendor's unique qualifications for your particular purpose should be included in the agreement, as that description will demonstrate your understanding of their expertise, and their understanding of your purpose in hiring them.

Scope of Provided Services

The provisions pertaining to the scope of service to be provided, are typically the "heart" of the agreement. Who will be doing what by when? How will they be accomplishing the work contemplated? Will there be sub-contractors? Is there a special licensing required to provide the service, or complete the contract?

Consideration

Consideration is a vital contract term, as any contract can be voided without sufficient consideration, but the term can be a little confusing. Consideration reflects what will be exchanged by both parties as part of the agreement. What compensation will be paid in exchange for the services provided? Will there be an exchange of money, or an exchange of services? How will payment be made, and by when? What happens if payment is late, or never arrives? Will interest accrue?

Term

To avoid perpetual agreements, it's important to ensure there is a "term" set in any contract, or provisions made for termination of the agreement under certain circumstances. So, what is the effective date? How long is the agreement to be in effect? Does it renew automatically? What happens if the agreement is terminated?

Jurisdiction and Choice of Law

Contracts should have provisions regarding where a potential lawsuit would be brought in the event of a dispute between the parties. Pay attention to this provision, as it may obligate you to respond to a lawsuit in a state far away from where you are located, and to hire legal counsel in the other state.

Further, it's important to note that while the nonprofit corporation may have been formed and established in one state, and it should benefit from the laws of that home state, contract terms can modify what state laws the parties wish to apply in any contract dispute. Oftentimes more established businesses and vendors have choice of law provisions in states with statutes that are more amenable to their position, and less friendly to yours.

Dispute Resolution

The default for any perceived breach of a contract is to file suit in court to enforce the provisions of the agreement, or to obtain a judgment for damages suffered by the non-breaching party. Lawsuits are expensive, time-consuming, and can take your time and attention away from what you really need to be doing as you grow a new organization. Thus, you may wish to consider provisions that would require mandatory mediation or arbitration, which can offer quicker, more efficient, and less costly alternatives to litigation.

Indemnification

The word "indemnity" has been derived from the original Latin term "indemnis," which means unhurt, or to be free from loss. Indemnification clauses in contracts are meant to protect one party from liability if a third-party or third entity is harmed in any way. It's a clause that contractually obligates one party to compensate another party for losses or damages that have occurred or could occur in the future.

In the nonprofit setting, a typical contract for rental of an event space for a fundraising event will typically have an indemnification provision in the contract, stating that the user (the nonprofit) shall indemnify the lessor of the facility for damage caused by their guests, or injuries to those guests. The indemnity clause is often paired, then, with a proof of insurance clause, often requiring a minimum of $1,000,000 in insurance coverage carried by the nonprofit.

We have now covered the primary obstacles that face you as you start a nonprofit organization, and the risks related to fundraising, governance, and IRS regulations. At this point, you may be tempted to think starting a new nonprofit is just too overwhelming. If this is the case, I would encourage you to continue reading. Understanding the challenges is just the first step; now it's time to chart your course through them!

Section 2 | Charting the Course

"Rarely are opportunities presented to you in a perfect way. In a nice little box with a yellow bow on top. 'Here, open it, it's perfect. You'll love it.' Opportunities - the good ones - are messy, confusing and hard to recognize. They're risky. They challenge you."
— Susan Wojcicki, CEO of YouTube

Now you understand the basic legal, financial, operational and regulatory hurdles you face; you have envisioned the change you wish to make in the world, and you understand the risks associated with making that change.

Now, it's time to chart your course.

The decision to start a new nonprofit organization is, to be sure, an opportunity; for you, and for your broader community. While it's difficult to determine exactly how you will implement the strategies needed for success, and there will be challenges along the way, there **is** a path to success that others have taken before you.

Over the past twenty years, I have helped hundreds of nonprofit founders to establish and grow new nonprofit organizations, and I've advised countless others in helping them to correct their governance, ensure they are fundraising in compliance with federal and state law, assess risk related to employment matters, and cure deficiencies and delinquencies in their compliance filings. I've observed how, and why, nonprofit organizations fail, and defended them when they are sued, audited, or threatened with sanctions and closure by the Internal Revenue Service, or state attorneys general.

As described in Chapter 1, the most successful nonprofit organizations that I have worked with over the decades have been ones that took the time to first understand the challenges and risks of starting a new nonprofit organization - like you have just done. Then, the organizations that will truly flourish are the ones that take the time to focus their time and attention in five primary areas: *Concept, Communications, Cash, Compliance* and *Culture.*

Chapter 6 | Concept

"Charting your own course isn't just more necessary than ever before. It's also much easier -

and much more fun."
- P!nk

Frame Your Success

The primary reason nonprofit organizations fail is their failure to plan. To be successful, then, prior to launching the new organization, the founder must first frame their success.

Twenty years ago, when I first started working with nonprofit organizations, there were few resources readily available to nonprofit founders and organizations about how to start and lead a nonprofit organization. Years later, an almost overwhelming number of resources and "guides" became available all over the internet, holding a fair amount of conflicting information.

That's one reason why, as a new nonprofit Executive Director in 2007, I decided to study and obtain a masters degree in Nonprofit Leadership and Management from the University of San Diego's

School of Leadership and Education Sciences; I
believed it was important to learn actual best practice,
rather than getting derailed by adopting poor
guidance provided by fly-by-night "advisors," or
documents I could find using a Google search.

Today, as back in 2007, excellent resources are
accessible and available on nonprofit leadership and
management. You've likely noticed; there are
thousands and thousands of websites, blogs, articles
and books on the subject.

The challenge, then, becomes how to sift through the
available material out there, and navigate through
what can seem like an overwhelming amount of
confusing, conflicting, and downright *bad* information
in order to decide how to proceed.

Thus, I believe that the best way to do that is to "frame
your success."

What do I mean by that? Well, think about the types of
photos and mementos you choose to display in your
home. These items could be treasured photos from
family vacations, the gap-toothed smiles of children or
grandchildren, or lovely pieces of art painted by your
favorite artist.

Each framed and featured item showcases your priorities, your values, and your aesthetic, demonstrating where you feel most comfortable and at peace.

Charting the course for this new nonprofit endeavor is no different; you must consciously select the features and critical elements this new organization must possess. At the outset, take the time to deliberately frame and feature the most important priorities and elements of your endeavor, and chart your course to achieve your goals.

Then - decide what you want to frame that purpose in? Will the plastic frame with cardboard foundation that came with your purchase do the trick? Or, do you think it might be best to seek out the best possible quality frame, that might cost a little bit more to obtain, to house your endeavor?

Remember, you are building something that will change the world; a cheap foundation will set your new organization up for quick failure.

Frame Your Purpose

Mother Teresa once said: *"We know only too well that what we are doing is nothing more than a drop in the ocean. But if the drop were not there, the ocean would be missing something."*

Purpose, even if it is only a single drop in a vast ocean, is at the heart of every nonprofit organization. It's why, when founding my nonprofit focused law firm over a decade ago, I chose the name **For Purpose Law Group**. It always surprised me that the accepted name for an entire, vibrant sector of the United States economy was taken from what it is **not**, rather than what it **actually is**.

Your organization is focused on your purpose, not on the fact that at the end of the year you do not distribute profits to shareholders. Indeed, your entire goal is to serve and "profit" your communities each and every day of the year.

Clearly describing and focusing upon exactly what you are focused on achieving, your specific purpose, then, is critical to the overall success of your nonprofit organization. When crafting your purpose statement, keep that in mind. This statement, or mission, will chart your course; it should include elements reflecting your core values and your vision for success.

Choose a Relevant (But Not Infringing) Name

Oftentimes, as part of a nonprofit founder's initial preception (as described in Chapter 1), they will have developed a firm idea of what they wish to name their new nonprofit organization. Before any name gets too ingrained in your psyche, however, I would encourage you to do a preliminary search of that name to determine if it is already being used by another organization or entity to avoid a false start before the gun fires at the starting line.

This search can be as simple as conducting a Google, Bing or other online search, or as complex as a comprehensive, global trademark search conducted by a law firm like For Purpose Law Group. If you find another organization that is already using that name, you likely will wish to reconsider using it, and perhaps select another. Why? Well, in the United States it's likely that the other organization, because it started using the name before you did, has acquired something known as "common law" trademark rights to use the name, and to shut down competing use of what they and others consider a "trademark" or "service mark" identifying their organization and services.

It's tempting to think that if your operations are contained to the city of Akron, Ohio, for example, it likely won't matter if you have a similar name to another organization doing similar work to you headquartered in Seattle, Washington. This is simply not the case; you'll likely receive a "cease and desist" letter from the first user of the mark - which, as you can imagine, can derail a new organization right when it's starting to gain traction.

After conducting your search, and determining that there is little likelihood of your chosen name infringing upon another organization's mark, then you very well may wish to consider preemptively protecting your name by filing a federal trademark application with the United States Patent and Trademark Office (USPTO). Because the USPTO conducts a full examination of your application prior to issuing a formal registration, obtaining that federal trademark registration is prima facie evidence that you have preemptive rights to use that mark over all subsequent users throughout the United States, and you will then be the one to send those warning letters to users who begin using the mark after you do.

Frame Your Core Values

One of my favorite quotes is one from Roy Bennett: *"There are some values that you should never compromise on to stay true to yourself; you should be brave to stand up for what you truly believe in, even if you stand alone."*

Most founders in this day and age understand the importance of an organization's core values. A good set of core values will provide a strong guiding light that can bond a nonprofit's team with a shared sense of purpose for what is important, and how the organization can achieve its goals, while also weathering the storms that will inevitably arise.

A good set of core values defines the organization's "why," and they inoculate the nonprofit organization's culture like a good vaccine, ensuring the long term health of the organization.

A bad set of core values, however, can sink a fledgling nonprofit organization quicker than anything else..

Don't think that if you neglect to actually set core values they will not exist; core values exist whether you set them intentionally, or not. A nonprofit founder can choose to proactively cultivate and nurture intentional core values from the very beginning or, much like a weed, the organization's core values will develop haphazardly (and often negatively) on their own over time through the inherent beliefs and different experiences of those on the team.

Thus, framing an organization's core values from the very start is critically important, and those values must be more than simply creating a list of guiding principles. Indeed, nonprofit organizations that authentically define how their team members operate, behave, and interact with both internal and external stakeholders from their inception are incredibly more successful than their counterparts.

Simply put, the time a nonprofit founder puts into defining, and nurturing a healthy organizational culture with defined core values will supercharge their organizational growth and ensure long-term health for their organization, enabling the nonprofit to not only flourish, but to also better weather the inevitable challenges any new nonprofit organization will face.

Frame Your Governance Structure

Not all nonprofit organizations have a corporate structure; some are organized as unincorporated associations, cooperatives, or trusts. These structures are relatively rare, however, and - in the case of unincorporated associations, for example, provide absolutely no protection to individual managers from the debts and liabilities of the organization, like a nonprofit corporate structure does. Thus, for the vast majority of new nonprofit organizations, a corporate structure is best and thus articles of incorporation as well as a board of directors is required.

Traditional Board Models: Governing, Working, and Advisory

Governance has been loosely defined as the processes, structures and organizational traditions that determine how power is exercised within an organization, how stakeholders communicate both externally and internally, and how decisions are made.

A "governing" board, then, is the traditional style of board governance, with the board overseeing the operations of the nonprofit organization by periodically meeting to evaluate the financial and operational health and the strategic direction of the organization. This style separates governance and management, leaving overall daily operations of the organization to the CEO / Executive Director and their staff.

A "working" board, on the other end of the spectrum, is expected to do quite a bit more. Most nonprofit organizations just getting started must, due to simple necessity, recruit "working" directors as the nonprofit has little to no staff to do the work that must be done. A working board, then, often finds itself "in the weeds," focused on the developing the systems, programs, services, and operations of a new nonprofit, leaving little time to envision and define the direction of the organization or evaluate the opportunities that may be available.

For organizations with a strong working board, then, it may be appropriate to consider establishing an "advisory" board. An advisory board is not a real "board," in that the members are not responsible for governance or management of the organization. Instead, their purpose is to focus their attention on the high-level opportunities and threats to the organization, ensuring that the fiduciary board members have the information, insight and guidance they need to move the organization forward.

Oftentimes advisory board members are experienced practitioners or "thought leaders" in a particular field, or they have successfully founded, grown and led a similar organization in the past. The knowledge and experience attained by these types of individuals can be incredibly useful to a working board, helping them to become established and fully functional in less time.

Opportunities for Creativity

While certain governance practices are legally required, such as maintaining good corporate records and ensuring directors understand their fiduciary duties, actual "governance" can be unique and strategically adapted to reflect your core values, and how your organization desires to operate.

Contrary to what most people think, nonprofit organizations can develop a governance structure, and a mixture of governance practices that uniquely suit them. This makes sense, when you think about it. Typical and traditional corporate governance structures and practices were crafted and developed for for-profit businesses, reporting to shareholders about how the corporation's executive team has maximized the value of the corporation, benefiting the shareholders who had invested in it.

We've already established that nonprofit organizations are different; they need to adapt the traditional model to reflect who they are, in order to be able to achieve their goals. When deciding how to govern themselves, nonprofit founders and directors should consider adopting some form of "generative governance."

Generative governance is a term coined by Richard Chait and his colleagues in the nonprofit governance text, *Governance as Leadership: Reframing the Work of Nonprofit Boards*.[2] In it, they describe a board that challenges itself, optimizes its performance, fosters innovation, and enhances stakeholder engagement; to think outside the box and to explore important societal challenges in new and different ways.

In my general counsel practice, for example, when providing guidance to my clients who are seeking to explore options outside the traditional, solely-compliance-focused governance models, I try to encourage them to think critically, craft new models that work for their unique circumstance, engage in strategic conversations, and harness their collective wisdom to develop the most effective governance structure for their organization.

A Model of Representative Governance

An example of generative governance in the nonprofit setting is one of constituent representation.

---

[2] Chait, Richard P.; Ryan, William P.; Taylor, Barbara E. (2011). Governance as Leadership. Hoboken, NJ: Wiley.

California's regional centers, a network of 21 community-based nonprofits, is a vibrant representative governance model, led by the Association of Regional Center Agencies (ARCA). The regional centers coordinate services for, and advocate on behalf of, nearly 400,000 Californians with developmental disabilities.

ARCA's Board is governed by representatives of each of the 21 nonprofits, and baked into their governance structure is a dedication to place adults with developmental disabilities and their family members as board directors, not just consumers of their services. After all, who understands the challenges facing this particular community better? Adults with developmental disabilities lead and inform this organization as it serves the community.

At a recent presentation that I conducted for the directors of ARCA's member organizations, one of the developmentally disabled director-participants shared how his leadership role not only accommodated his disability but also fulfilled his goals to bring what he has learned to improve his Native American community.

Traditional corporate directorships, in a traditional governance model, wouldn't work for ARCA; their unique form of governance, however, does.

A Model of Minimum Governance

The prolific nonprofit blogger, Vu Le, has declared the traditional corporate board model archaic and toxic. He laments the traditions that have been passed down that most believe are legally required, even though they are not. He asks, *"The board hires the ED. Who says?! The board meets once a month. Why?! The board approves the budget. Not necessarily!"*

A nonprofit board on which he sits, "Creating the Future," for example, is exploring a governance structure that includes something he terms a "minimally viable board," where a small board fulfills the absolute minimum legal requirements, ensures compliance, and does little else.

Then, they are creating a second, less formal but much larger, more expansive, more inclusive (and more fun, I would imagine) "integrity board" that reflects the community it serves, and that community's values.

A Model of Evolutionary Governance

Another unique governance model is one utilized by Dream Rider Productions, which has described this model as one of *Evolutionary Governance*. This model is focused on equality in both form and function. It includes the board and staff sharing corporate power, as well as the board being a supportive partner and sounding board for the Executive Director.

For example, the board does nothing if "nothing" is what is needed at various moments, resulting in increased time for everyone to do a lot of inner work.

They understand the minimum legal requirements the board must meet, ensure it's quickly outsourced or completed, and then they focus their attention on much more interesting things.

At this point, I do need to take off my "nonprofit leadership" hat, and put on my "nonprofit lawyer" one. While I highly encourage generative governance structures, before fully implementing a non-traditional structure, consulting with an experienced nonprofit attorney is critical. There are several corporate provisions, which can vary by state, that can not be changed or waived even if you wanted to do so.

Frame Your Measures of Success

The traditional methods of measuring success, utilized by many for-profit businesses, are solely quantitative in nature, and do not translate well when gauging the impact and reach of many nonprofit organizations. What I mean by "quantitative" is that most businesses, for example, tend to measure growth and success utilizing objective numbers; profit, employee headcount, or the business' appeal to potential buyers and shareholders for example.

Measuring success within most nonprofit organizations, however, must be much more nuanced.

Nonprofit organizations must measure their success using both quantitative **and qualitative** measures in order to demonstrate their true impact and success.

Creating Your Own Unique Measurements

At the very beginning of an organization's life-cycle, it's critical to establish your own unique, clear and measurable criteria for success, identifying any specific data points that will measure your progress towards the goals you've set.

Once you've established that criteria, you should develop and map out the systems you will need in order to collect the data you have identified that you will need to demonstrate either program success, or program failure. These measures should be a mix of both quantitative and qualitative data, as well as an analysis of both.

Quantitative data is numbers-based, countable, or measurable. This type of data describes how many, how much, or how often when calculating success. It's fixed, and empirical; it's measuring, counting and calculating numbers.

For example, if your organization is focused on improving youth literacy rates, you may collect data reflecting the number of students reading at or above grade level. Additional examples of qualitative measures include the number of hungry people served at your food bank, how many diabetic children were able to attend their first summer camp due to your efforts, or how many homeless pets were placed in loving homes by your organization over the past year.

Quantitative data measures are relatively quick and easy to collect, and they are relatively easy to use in determining programmatic success. Interpreting the quantitative data you've collected, and communicating your successes is straightforward, and is less subjective or open to multiple interpretations.

However, quantitative data doesn't always tell your full story, or demonstrate true success. Quantitative data often overlooks our human nature, and broader themes or progress. By focusing solely on numbers, there is a risk of missing unique information that can be beneficial.

Qualitative measures of success, then, can become extremely useful. They are interpretation-based, descriptive, and unique in they can help you understand why, how, or what happened due to certain behaviors. Typically, qualitative research methods require interviewing and observing stakeholders, and recording responses and grouping data into categories and themes.

When advising my clients in determining how best to measure the success of their overall mission, and the programs they have implemented to reach their vision, I encourage nonprofit leaders to consider not only hard data impact such as number of people they have served over the course of the program or the year, but also to measure and track data related to more subjective successes, including resource mobilization, staff effectiveness, organizational reputation or perceived community benefits that will better demonstrate their true impact

Chapter 7 | Communication

"Good communication is the bridge
between confusion and clarity."
— Nat Turner.

As we discussed in Chapter 3, when it comes to
maintaining an organization's classification as a public
charity, rather than being classified as a private
foundation, it's critically important that the financial
support of the public is sought and maintained. That
means that the nonprofit must inform potential
donors, volunteers, stakeholders and other
community members about their mission, vision,
programs and services in such a way that will inspire
continued, long-lasting support for the organization.

Creating a communications plan, then, is incredibly
important to the success of an organization, and
should include multiple methods crafted to distribute
information describing the organization's mission,
vision and goals as well as how it measures
programmatic impact and success. All of your
communications should be well-thought-out, and
carefully crafted in order to appeal to potential donors
as well as recruit active volunteers or employees, in
order to meet programmatic goals.

Craft Your Case

We've already explored the importance of knowing, and describing your purpose. Now, it's time to utilize that purpose and mission statement to focus on some specific communications that will need to be crafted to convey your **why** to various internal and external stakeholders.

Author and thought-leader Simon Sinek has the fourth most-viewed TED Talk of all time, with over 43 million views, and another 10 million views on YouTube. This talk, filmed in 2009 entitled *"How Great Leaders Inspire Action,"* expounds upon the topic of finding your purpose, or your *"why."* He stated, *"People don't buy what you do; they buy **why you do it** and what you do simply proves what you believe. In fact, people will do the things that prove what they believe."*

You might be thinking that your organization won't be selling anything, but that is simply not the case. Your organization *is* selling hope, and the idea of making a positive social or community change. In essence, you are "in the business" of inspiring others to take action.

Oftentimes, nonprofit organizations utilize a core set of communications to inspire others, and these communications are called a *Case for Support*, a *Case*

Statement or a *Donor Prospectus*, depending largely upon how your organization plans to raise funds.

While most applicable to organizations whose primary funding mechanism are gifts, grants or donations, it's never a bad idea to have drafted a robust case for support even if your primary revenue is derived from fees you charge participants.

Case Summary

Sit down and start drafting, and explaining your purpose, including what your organization is trying to accomplish, and why it matters. Explain what is needed in the way of funds, time, effort, etc. to grow your impact.

It's tempting to start with your history, and lead off with "The nonprofit was founded in 2020 by Joe and Nancy Thomas..." Don't do that. You'll lose the reader's interest almost immediately. Open with an emotional statement, one that grabs the reader, and makes them want to read more. From the very start, your Case for Support should make the reader *feel* a response to what you have written.

Your Mission and Vision

After you've "hooked" the reader with your opening, it's time to move on to the reasons your organization exists. What challenges are you trying to solve? What are the gaps in services or resources that you have observed? What does success look like to you?

Programs & Services

Explain exactly how your organization is different. Illustrate your proposed impact, and describe how you will be measuring the data that will inform your success going forward. Utilize as much impact data, and as many stories or quotes from the people who will benefit from your programs and services as possible.

History of the Organization

Start building your history. As a new organization, you don't have much in the way of past history or data to utilize in showcasing your successes, so you will need to help your supporters, volunteers, and donors understand the genesis of your organization, and in what direction you are confidently headed.

Because you don't have your own data, yet, utilize the data from other organizations that have gone before you. Gather the relevant or ancillary data on their success, and then demonstrate how you can meet or exceed those results.

Your Impact

Any donor that is potentially interested in supporting your organization will want to know that if they decide to support you, their contribution will make a real difference. Utilize the data you decided to track as described in Chapter 6. Finally, tell the stories of the people you have served; use testimonials provided by community leaders, supporters, and your biggest fans. Convince the reader of how important his or her contribution to you will be!

Financial Needs & Request for Support

It's now time to talk about money, and what you are hoping to garner in the way of financial support. Be specific. Describe exactly what the money will be used for, and how it will impact the community that you serve. If you are able, consider relating a specific donated amount to your mission and proposed impact.

Using the example of Humanity Showers, again, in their case for support they could describe that a donation of $1,000 will provide 200 showers and 50 haircuts to homeless men and women seeking employment, and a path out of poverty ... $15,000 would provide another shower trailer, enabling them to serve thousands more... and $25,000 would provide much-needed equipment and supplies enabling them to serve an additional county in need.

Communicate Your Impact

Once you have crafted your case for support, it's important to determine how you will communicate the success you will be achieving.

Since 2018, Coastal Roots Farm, a nonprofit organization located in Encinitas, California, has crafted both quarterly and annual reports, posted them on their website, and distributed them throughout social media.

The Farm's mission is to cultivate healthy, connected communities by integrating sustainable agriculture, food justice, and ancient Jewish wisdom. They do this by educating the public on the practice of organic farming, sharing the resultant harvest with the disadvantaged, and fostering "inclusive spaces for people of all ages and backgrounds to come together to celebrate Jewish life and catalyze a healthier, more vibrant community and a more sustainable future for the region." Check them out, here:
https://coastalrootsfarm.org/our-story/

As a result of the record-breaking precipitation that hit California during the winter of 2023, in just the first three months of the year more rain had fallen than during the entire previous year. This increase in precipitation resulted in a huge harvest... of weeds.

The gardeners at Coastal Roots Farm, however, knew that these weeds were edible, and they were nutrient-dense. These included nettle, chrysanthemum, wild mustard and wild spinach, that they determined that they were able to utilize in their *Organic Food Distribution Program*. Over those first three months of the year, the Farm was able to extend their impact and serve more people than they ever had before.

In their report for the 2nd quarter of 2023, they featured this unusual programmatic success in addition to their traditional measures of organizational impact, which typically includes how many eggs were laid by their chickens, how many pounds of food were grown on the farm, and how many people they were able to feed during the quarter.

It's important to develop consistent and relevant messaging like this, and to practice communicating how your organization is living its mission, working towards achieving its vision, and reaching measurable goals that have been set for its success as described in your original case for support.

Your Website Domain

Now it's time to consider purchasing an internet domain, and setting up an email service. While it's possible to create a free email account in many online services, establishing a professional website and affiliated email addresses should be one of your first "non-programmatic" expenditures.

Having a website allows your organization to convey your messaging, and engage stakeholders, better than any other method of communication. When choosing and purchasing your domain, you may wish to look for and purchase domains with both .com and .org suffixes available. This will help prevent a competitor, or other new organization that does understand trademark rights, to set up shop using the same name, but with a different suffix. It's worth the cost to lock down both.

Services like GoDaddy.com, Google Workspace, Wix and Wordpress all offer reasonable website and email services, and depending upon your goals and objectives, one of their established templates can get you up and running extremely quickly.

It's often tempting to set up emails for your board, volunteers, and other workers based on their role or position, such as president@yourdomain.org, or volunteercoordinator@yourdomain.org. It would seem to be a good idea to enable a new president or worker to have access to past communications, or to always ensure that information that needs to go to the president, for example, will always go to the president (whoever that may be at any given time).

Before making that decision, however, think about if that person will need to be signing documents electronically, or if multiple people will have access to that email account. Shared and "passed down" accounts can lead to invalid or challengeable signatures on documents, causing more headaches down the road than the initial reason for setting up the emails in this fashion were meant to solve.

A good IT company can set you up with individual email accounts as well as shared email accounts, if appropriate, to be used when there will be multiple people that need access. This is a low-cost, reality-based option that sets you up for success.

Social Media

There are almost 4 billion social media users worldwide, and that number is constantly growing. Many people use social media platforms like Facebook, TikTok or Instagram not only to keep up with friends, but they also use these platforms to engage with their favorite causes and organizations.

Nonprofits, by establishing a presence on social media, can host fundraisers, recruit volunteers, and convey relevant stories that can inspire and grow support.

As one caveat to the "shared" email warning, above, we recommend that you create at least one, centrally used email address, that can be used to establish social media accounts and other online accounts like Zoom, phone services like RingCentral, or document storage master accounts, rather than an email address linked to a specific person.

Oftentimes, new organizations will ask a volunteer or director to set up these accounts, and they will use their personal login credentials to do so. If there is a "falling out," or argument with that individual, we've seen accounts belonging to a nonprofit organization held hostage by the individuals who originally set up the accounts.

Thus, we typically recommend setting up your own domain, and using generic usernames, such as "info@yourdomain.org" or "programs@yourdomain.org" for this purpose. We do not recommend using "admin@yourdomain.org" as online cyber attacks typically focus on gaining access to your accounts using "admin@yourdomain.org" as their prime target.

It's important, too, to draft and adopt a Social Media Communications Policy, reflecting not only the types of content that will best help the organization achieve its goal, but also what rules and guidelines must be followed when those tasked with posting content do so.

Social Media Communications Policy

We have a template Social Media Communications Policy on our website which we've made available for you to download.

www.nonprofitcounsel.com/start-a-nonprofit-change-the-world-resources

Email Communications

As soon as possible, you should begin collecting the email addresses of your supporters, stakeholders, friends and family. Sending out email communications will keep those people informed about the work the nonprofit organization does, as well as advertise volunteer or fundraising events, and solicit support in the way of financial contributions or non-cash donations.

Whether you're looking to increase engagement or drive donations, communicating to your supporters via email is one of the most effective methods of doing so. Consider tasking a volunteer possessing great communication skills with drafting and sending a weekly or monthly newsletter to start. Have an "opt in" form on your website, and invite all of your friends and family to subscribe.

Your organization can utilize your email service and a large "bcc" email list, or there are several online services that will facilitate the gathering and use of an email list for a fee; among those we've seen are Constant Contact, Mail Chimp, and Active Campaign.

Tax Filings, Reports, and Receipts as Part of Your Communications Plan

Every tax-exempt organization must complete, on an annual basis, an informational tax return for filing with the IRS which, like any for-profit business return, includes information on income, expenses, and assets.

Savvy nonprofit organizations utilize this required annual filing as a critically important part of their overall communications plan. After all, prior to donating to an organization many individual donors will consult popular online services such as Candid to review an organization's past returns to gauge how impactful their contributions will be.

Further, when applying for grants provided by private or communication foundations, those grant making organizations typically consult past returns to ensure good financial management on the part of the public charity.

Unlike a traditional business return, the Form 990 tax filing not only includes pointed questions related to governance, related party transactions, and foreign activities, it also asks about the nonprofit's three largest programs based upon expenditures, and it provides an area specifically designed for an organization to describe how their programs have impacted the community, and to demonstrate their success over the past year. Further, every nonprofit is able to include an additional narrative of their successes, utilizing the Schedule O.

Finally, all nonprofit organizations that accept charitable donations must provide to any donor (who gives more than $250 to them) a "contemporaneous written receipt," memorializing the contribution to be used to substantiate any deduction the donor makes on his or her individual tax return. "Contemporaneous" has been interpreted by the Internal Revenue Service to mean "within the tax year." Thus, most savvy nonprofit organizations use this IRS requirement as part of their year end fundraising appeal, providing the required donation receipt, and *at the same time* asking for additional financial support during the month of December, when traditional giving to charity is at its peak.

Call Others to Action

Now it's time to put the pieces all together, and seek support. Many nonprofit founders find this incredibly difficult, but it doesn't have to be! People are innately wired to wish to make a difference to others; to volunteer their time and resources to things that are important to them, whether that is their local church community or contributing to the battle against climate change.

No matter what your charitable, educational, or religious purpose is, you will be able to find individual, and potentially institutional, donors who have an affinity for that purpose, and will wish to support your organization.

Opportunities for Volunteers

Humans are innately wired to want to solve problems, and be of assistance to others. As the founder of a new nonprofit organization, you will be able to utilize this desire to appeal to the people around you to contribute both expertise, and time. Recently, I presented to a group of aspiring nonprofit directors at a "board matching" program sponsored by the University of San Diego and the United Way of San Diego. Bankers, accountants, human resource professionals, academics, and even the mayor of a small Orange County town were in attendance, learning how they could best bring their talents and excitement for service to a deserving organization.

Seek out these types of volunteers, and call them to action by demonstrating how your organization can -

and will! - impact their lives, and their innate sense of purpose.

Opportunities for Financial Support

When you have completed your Case for Support you now have the ability to answer donors and supporters who ask the question, "so *what?*" Now, it's time to craft the message that you can use to respond to those who then say, "*now what?*"

For potential donors, you can now fine tune your "ask;" you can appeal for financial support from potential supporters, including community foundations, private foundations, and individual donors. Asking people for money is often an area of discomfort for many new founders who haven't done the work of crafting a compelling case. You'll find, however, that this activity becomes infinitely more comfortable once your case statement has been completed, and you have it in hand.

Advocacy and Lobbying

Leaders and managers of nonprofit organizations, both old and new, often believe that a nonprofit organization is precluded from lobbying and performing any advocacy work. They assume, perhaps based on the Johnson Amendment's prohibition of political campaign activity, that their tax-exempt status will be placed at risk if they conduct *any* legislative advocacy or lobbying.

This is simply not the case.

My good friend and mentor, who I first met when attending the University of San Diego during my nonprofit leadership and management master's program, is Pat Libby. She is one of the nation's leading experts on nonprofit lobbying, and has written several books on the subject including her most recent tome, "*The Empowered Citizens Guide: 10 Steps to Passing a Law that Matters to You.*"[3] She has made educating nonprofit leaders on not only their ability, but *on their duty* to lobby and advocate for the communities they serve, part of her professional life's mission.

She espouses, as do I, that no one is better able to advocate for the individuals and communities most in need of being heard by legislators (but being the least likely to be able to do so) than nonprofit organizations.

---

[3] Libby, P. (2022). *The Empowered Citizens Guide: 10 Steps to Passing a Law That Matters to You.* Oxford University Press.

From a legal standpoint, it is important for nonprofit organizations to understand how this type of lobbying activity is viewed by the Internal Revenue Service, and how it must be reported by the nonprofit. As we covered in Chapter 2, 501(c)(3) organizations must be organized and operated *exclusively* for exempt purposes.

Through decades of challenges and many revenue rulings, the IRS takes the position that as long as the lobbying is not a "substantial" part of the organization's activities, then the organization's tax exempt status is not at risk.

So, the question then becomes what does "substantial" mean?

The default meaning, in the eyes of the IRS, is a bit subjective. If they believe the organization is lobbying too much, they will apply a "facts and circumstances" test. The IRS will look at all sorts of things when evaluating your activities, *including the time spent by volunteers and employees*, as well as the money you've spent on any lobbying activities, and then make a determination based on their findings of whether or not the activity was "substantial."

Anytime the IRS can make a subjective determination using a "facts and circumstances" evaluation, it's incredibly difficult for a taxpayer to overcome.

But there is another option.

Public charities may elect to have their lobbying activities measured using an "expenditure test," which has the benefit of being an *objective* measure, rather than a subjective one.

Under the expenditure test, the extent of a nonprofit's lobbying activity will not jeopardize the organization's tax-exempt status, provided that the expenditures, related to such activity, do not normally exceed a certain threshold which varies by overall expenditures.

For charities with under $500,000 in annual expenditures, they are limited to expending <20% of that amount towards lobbying activities. For larger nonprofits, the rules get a little more complex, but generally these types of expenditures cannot exceed $1,000,000, even for the largest of nonprofit organizations.

As you can imagine, it's much better to have an objective measure to gauge your compliance with these IRS regulations than a subjective "facts and circumstances" test. Additionally, because this test *only measures expenditures*, your nonprofit can utilize the efforts of your volunteer stakeholders and supporters without issue.

Technically, all the nonprofit organization needs to do to opt out of the "default" measure, and make a "501(h) election" to apply the "expenditure test" to their activities, is to complete and submit a simple half page election form to the IRS (Form 5768).

Chapter 8 | Cash

"Money is of no value; it cannot spend itself.
All depends on the skill of the spender."
- Ralph Waldo Emerson

It's at this point in an organization's start-up journey that we begin receiving calls from nonprofit founders, asking for our assistance. When we first started For Purpose Law Group (FPLG), we did not offer accounting and bookkeeping services to our clients. However, because this phase is such a critical piece of an organization's initial and long-term success, we decided we had to begin counseling clients on their financial health in addition to their legal structure and requirements.

Developing a comprehensive financial plan is crucial for nonprofit founders to establish and operate a successful organization that will stand the test of time. Those that do not develop one, are more likely than not to fail. The financial plan serves as a roadmap for the organization's financial health, providing a clear picture of the nonprofit's financial position, goals, and strategies to achieve those goals.

The first step is to determine your method of accounting, and then craft your initial chart of accounts.

The second step is to craft your financial plan. This plan should include your organization's budget, including potential revenue streams, program expenses, and fundraising goals. This plan should demonstrate your organization's financial sustainability, and its ability to generate revenue.

During the course of my practice, I've seen nonprofit organizations sketch out their initial charts of account and budgets on napkins, on legal pads, excel spreadsheets or on a multitude of whiteboards.

How you do it is not important; it's just important that you *actually do it*.

Methods of Accounting

In accounting, there are two primary methods of tracking income and expenses: cash-basis accounting and accrual-basis accounting. When you apply for exempt status, for example, the IRS will ask you which method you will be utilizing and they will continue to ask about your methods on every subsequent 990-EZ or full 990 filing you submit to them.

Why does it even matter?

Well, the two different methods offer different financial reports that affect the way to determine the financial position of the nonprofit organization.

Cash-based accounting, for example, is based on what the name suggests. It is the simpler method of accounting, and transactions are recorded whenever you receive cash from donors, clients, or customers and whenever cash leaves your organization in the form of expenses or vendor payments.

Accrual-based accounting, on the other hand, is based not on when cash comes in or goes out, but when those transactions are *initiated*. In a nutshell, you record revenue when you earned it (even if you haven't received it, yet), and expenses when you incur them (even if you haven't paid them, yet).

Typically, for most organizations just getting started, we recommend selecting cash-based accounting for its simplicity, and its ability to provide an accurate picture of how much money there is in your nonprofit organization at any given time.

Regardless of what method you select, however, it's important that you do choose one over the other, and that you stick to that method unless and until it makes sense to change it.

Charts of Account

The foundation for effectively tracking and reporting their financial health and activities is a chart of accounts (COA). The COA is the backbone of all of your accounting procedures, and should be personalized to include everything you are planning to do financially. It provides a logical organizational structure for all of your financial information. Generally, the COA comprises five categories:

- **Assets.** What the organization owns, such as cash, investments, receivables (if you've chosen accrual-based accounting), and fixed assets.
- **Liabilities**. What the organization owes and - if you are using accrual-based accounting, include your payables, accrued expenses and deferred revenue.
- **Net Assets**. What the value of the organization's assets are minus the liabilities, showing the total financial value of the organization.

- **Income.** The revenue that the organization receives, from programming and fundraising to grants and investments.
- **Expenses.** The money the organization spends on salaries, payroll, rent, utilities, professional fees, and other costs to run the nonprofit.

There are a ton of resources out there for nonprofit organizations setting up their COAs. For example, if you do a simple search on Google, you'll likely find the *Unified Chart of Accounts (UCOA)*. This tool was created by the Financial Accounting Standards Board (FASB) as a standardized chart of accounts for nonprofit use, and it has the benefit of being easily translated directly and easily into the financial categories required by the IRS on the Form 990.

However, some have likened applying the full UCOA to a small organization as akin to killing a mosquito with a sledgehammer. It's incredibly detailed, and simply too massive and complex for most small nonprofits to wrap their head around. Thus, creating a custom COA that reflects how your organization will operate financially is the better option.

Assign and Organize Account Numbers

A COA is designed to be highly logical and organized, with the various accounts within your nonprofit chart of accounts designated with specific unique numbers. These numbers are then grouped to make it easier to find specific accounts as money is spent or received, which helps you to keep your COA organized.

When creating your COA account numbers, consider using the following guide:

1000 - Assets
2000 - Liabilities
3000 - Net Assets
4000 - Contributions
5000 - Earned Revenue
6000 - Other Income
7000 - Personnel Expenses
8000 - Non-Personnel Related Expenses

The COA account numbers will act as headers for a group of accounts. Then, within each of these designations, you'll create subcategories. For instance, you might list out the following subcategories within the overall "assets" category:

1010 - Checking

1020 - Savings
1030 - Accounts Receivable (if using accrual based accounting)
1040 - Investments
1050 - Equipment
1060 - Petty Cash
1070 - Other Assets

When you create these subcategories, try to group them together according to commonalities to help keep the chart of accounts well organized. For example, within the larger Revenue category, you might designate:

5010 - Donations and Grants from Individuals
5020 - Donations and Grants from Government Agencies
5030 - Donations and Grants from Private Foundations
5040 - Fundraising Sponsorships
5050 - Fundraising Ticket Sales
5060 - Fundraising Auction Sales

As you can see from the above list, donations and grants from various sources are grouped together, fundraising revenue is also grouped together, but there are enough subcategories listed to determine with some level of granularity where the various funding is coming from. This helps keep everything organized and legible throughout the nonprofit chart of accounts.

In addition, when you create your chart of accounts, try to leave some numbers free between the different subcategories and categories. This will allow you to add new accounts to the list in appropriate locations as your organization grows and evolves. For example, you might decide to add Fundraising from Raffle Sales, but you would want to include it alongside the fundraising from other sources. Therefore, it may be designated as 5055 to be sure it's included in the right location.

Doing the work at the beginning to properly categorize and organize your various financial accounts will save you, your board, your bookkeeper and your tax preparer a great deal of time and confusion in the long run.

Template Chart of Accounts

We have a free nonprofit chart of accounts excel template on our website which we've made available for you to download.

www.nonprofitcounsel.com/start-a-nonprofit-change-the-world-resources

Develop a Budget

A budget is the first, critical component of any financial plan. Indeed, on the *Form 1023 Application for Exemption from Income Tax*, if you do the full application rather than the 1023-EZ, the IRS asks for you to propose a three year budget for your organization, showing both anticipated revenue and projected expenses.

Good budgeting also helps you focus on the important strategic goals you set for your organization, and it will impact how you craft your case for support. After all, whether or not you can conduct a program or service is largely dependent upon the availability and timing of relevant funding.

Having a budget in place also ensures that your board is making informed decisions and providing guidance that is related to the setting financial goals, with relevant information. This reduces the occurrence of meetings where everyone is confused, and countless hours are spent trying to interpret your organization's financial information.

The key elements of a budget include revenue and expenses. Specifically, your budget will describe how your organization is planning on funding its programs throughout the fiscal year, and then how that money is anticipated to be spent on your programs and services in order to achieve your goals and mission.

Revenue & Fundraising

As part of developing your budget, first focus on revenue. It's important to remember that nonprofit organizations have many potential sources of revenue beyond just grants and donations, which are the typical revenue streams most people remember when thinking about how a nonprofit organization raises money.

Take the time to identify every possible potential source of revenue, including grants and donations, but also include fundraising events, fee-for-service or program fees, and ancillary methods including raffles, bingo, Amazon Smile, sponsorships, and other types of support. For purposes of your initial budget, you might find it easier to skip "non-cash" contributions, such as services or donated items and equipment.

Be realistic in your revenue projections, but also believe in yourself. Establishing a confident mindset, paired with strategic revenue projections can be transformative.

Earned Revenue

For example, the stated purpose of College Forward, an Austin-based nonprofit, is to coach underserved, yet motivated, students on how to obtain a college degree by showcasing the benefits of higher education. They conduct outreach and educational programs, but they also sell their curriculum and programming to partner organizations, utilizing their innovative technology platform, CoPilot, which was built on the Salesforce.com platform.

College Forward recognized that they had developed programmatic expertise, and had innovative methods of delivering that expertise that would be of value to others. They recognized they had something they already used, they realized it had commercial potential related to their purpose, and they are selling access to it, resulting in increased financial resources for their organization.

Expenses & Program Development

After you have completed mapping out all of the revenue your organization can expect to receive over time, then it's time to list out all expenses, such as salaries and benefits, program costs, administrative expenses, and fundraising expenses. It is crucial to ensure that the budget is realistic and achievable, and that projected revenues exceed expenses to ensure financial sustainability.

Monitoring expenses regularly is essential to ensure that the organization is operating within its budget. Nonprofit founders should regularly review financial statements and budget reports to identify overspending or potential cost savings. Nonprofit founders should also track financial metrics, such as cash flow and liquidity, to ensure financial sustainability.

Functional Expense Reporting

Nonprofit organizations will typically track expenses by their "function," which means tracking the money the nonprofit organization spends according to what the money was used for, like fundraising, operations, administration, or programs. This is a good practice to become accustomed to, as a "statement of functional expenses" is required on full Form 990 filings, which are required when an organization exceeds $200,000 on average in gross receipts. If you've tracked your functional expenses all year, it's not a hassle to transfer your financial information to your accountant or tax preparer at the end of the year.

Regular Financial Reporting

Once you've adopted your chart of accounts, and set your budget, it's time to start tracking the organization's financial health, and that is done by generating and reviewing financial information on a regular basis.

The most successful nonprofit organizations I have worked with have utilized reliable accounting software and systems to regularly track their financial activities and transactions in order to generate relevant and correct financial statements for internal stakeholders and directors to rely upon.

Further, when it comes time to ensure your organization remains in compliance with federal and state agencies, having the information up to date and easily utilized is key to accurate and timely tax return preparation and reporting. In our tax and accounting practice at FPLG, for example, we utilize Quickbooks Online for our clients, a software that allows for online, real-time collaboration and data analysis from Chief Financial Officers, Treasurers, Board Presidents to their accounting and tax advisors.

Typically, in addition to the Statement of Functional Expenses we covered earlier in this chapter, the financial reports that should be created and reviewed include a Statement of Activity (also known as a "profit and loss" statement), a Statement of Financial Position (also known as a "balance sheet"), a Statement of Cash Flows and a Statement of Functional Expenses, which shows how you are allocating and expending funds within various programs.

I am often asked how often an organization should generate these financial reports. My answer is that, at minimum, the organization should provide financial reports to the board of directors, each time they meet. This will enable them to not only fulfill their fiduciary duties to the organization, but can allow them to identify potential areas of financial concern before they reach a critical level.

Responsibilities to Donors

A nonprofit organization should, as part of its gift acceptance policy, have in place a procedure for providing donors not only a sincere "thank you!" for their gift, but also a written acknowledgement reflecting the particulars of the donation.

As we discussed in Chapter 7, in order for a donor to deduct a charitable contribution of $250 or more made to your organization, they must have a contemporaneous, written acknowledgment of that donation from you - and they must maintain it in case they are ever audited by the Internal Revenue Service.

As for what needs to be included in that acknowledgement, well - it must include the following:

1. The name of the nonprofit organization;
2. The amount of cash contribution (if the donation was cash);
3. A description (but **not** the value) of any non-cash contribution, which could include stock, cryptocurrency, artwork, equipment, or any other tangible property;
4. A statement that *"no goods or services were provided by the organization in return for the contribution"*, if that is the case;
5. If it wasn't, then a description and good faith estimate of the value of goods or services, if any, that the organization *did* provide in return for the contribution, if you did provide anything in return;
6. A statement that goods or services, if any, that the organization provided in return for the contribution consisted entirely of intangible religious benefits (if that was the case).

While it isn't technically necessary to include your Federal Employer Identification Number on the written acknowledgment, most nonprofit organizations tend to do so, to make it easier on the donor to substantiate the organization's tax exempt status.

Template Donor Acknowledgment

We have a free nonprofit donor acknowledgment on our website which we've made available for download.

www.nonprofitcounsel.com/start-a-nonprofit-change-the-world-resources

Chapter 9 | Compliance

"Let's make it simple: Government control means uniformity, regulation, fees, inspection, and yes, compliance."
- Tom Graves

Nonprofit organizations, like their for-profit counterparts, are required to abide by federal, state, and local regulations. Unlike traditional businesses, however, nonprofit 501(c)(3) charities have a slew of additional requirements, including adopting required policies applicable to nonprofit organizations, operating in such a way as to maintain the organization's tax-exempt status, and completing annual registration and charity registration filings.

As a nonprofit attorney, I have witnessed the unwavering passion and dedication that countless nonprofit leaders bring to their missions. Enthusiasm serves as a driving force, but it is equally crucial for organizations to remain compliant with legal and regulatory requirements in order to continue making a positive impact on their communities, and the world.

Required Nonprofit Policies

There are four governance policies that the IRS Form 990 asks whether a charitable nonprofit has adopted:

- ☐ Written conflict of interest policy (Part VI, Section B, Line 12);
- ☐ Written whistleblower protection policy (Part VI, Section B, line 13);
- ☐ Written document retention and destruction policy (Part VI, Section B, line 14);
- ☐ Written gift acceptance policy that governs the receipt of "non-cash" gifts, such as gifts-in-kind, and unusual gifts (land, vehicles, artwork, conservation easements, etc.).

According to the IRS, "*A conflict of interest policy is intended to help ensure that when actual or potential conflicts of interest arise, the organization has a process in place under which the affected individual will advise the governing body about all the relevant facts concerning the situation.*"

Contrary to what many people think, conflicts of interest are not forbidden per se; conflicts can exist, be disclosed to the full board, and dealt with appropriately by establishing procedures under which individuals who have a conflict of interest will be excused from voting on the matters in which they have a conflict, resulting in the decision being made by a majority of disinterested directors on the nonprofit board.

This is why, as we discussed in Chapter 2, I typically advise new organizations to elect three unrelated and disinterested board members, so that if there is a conflict with one director, the two remaining directors can evaluate and assess the proposed transaction.

Thereafter, if both directors elect to accept and ratify the proposed transaction, those two directors reflect a majority decision and can pass a valid board resolution regarding the transaction. If, however, one of the other members was related to the member with a conflict of interest, there is no way to evaluate the transaction – and the remaining director cannot pass a valid board action with two "excused" directors.

Sample Core Governance Policies

Conflict of Interest Policy: Required by the Internal
Revenue Service

Whistleblower Protection Policy: Required under
Sarbannes-Oxley

Document Retention and Destruction Policy: Required
under Sarbannes-Oxley

Gift Acceptance Policy: Required by the Internal
Revenue Service

We have free templates of these four policies on our
website which we've made available for download.

www.nonprofitcounsel.com/start-a-nonprofit-
change-the-world-resources

Maintaining Tax-Exempt Status

To maintain tax-exempt status once you have received it, nonprofit organizations must continue to observe the rules we covered in Chapter 2. Specifically, the nonprofit organization must:

- Continue to be "Organized" and "Operated" for tax-exempt purposes;
- Ensure that their activities and resources do not "inure" to the benefit of private individuals or interests;
- Limit unrelated business activity and lobbying activity to ensure they are no more than "insubstantial."

In addition, an organization that has received tax exempt status, other than those recognized as churches, are required to annually complete and file an informational tax return (Form 990, 990-EZ, or 990-N) depending upon the organization's gross receipts and year end assets. Failure to do so for three consecutive years will result in *automatic* revocation of the organization's tax exempt status.

Charitable Solicitation

Nonprofits that solicit charitable contributions are subject to federal and state fundraising regulations. The IRS requires organizations to disclose certain information to donors, such as the tax-deductibility of contributions and any goods or services provided in exchange for donations. Additionally, individual states may enforce their own rules governing fundraising practices, which include registration with state regulators, financial reporting, and disclosure requirements.

Uniform Registration Statement (URS)

The URS reflects the efforts of the National Association of State Charities Officials and the National Association of Attorneys General, to standardize, simplify, and economize compliance under various states' solicitation laws.

The URS effort is now in version 4.0 of the form, which is accepted by thirty-seven of the forty jurisdictions requiring registration. Reflecting this dynamic, the URS is updated continually by way of its website. See Item #6 in the "Reminders" section (URS Instructions, pg. 4) for more information on URS packet updates.

To ensure you have access to the latest version of the URS, please visit: http://multistatefiling.org/, or use the QR code, below.

Lobbying and Political Campaign Activity

As discussed in Chapter 7, it's well within the purview of nonprofit organizations to lobby and be advocates for the communities and individuals they serve. Indeed, it's something that every nonprofit should evaluate.

It would be shortsighted, however, to think there are no risks associated with this activity. In other words, advocacy is a critically important function, but a nonprofit leader should understand the compliance boundaries of actively lobbying, and ensure the nonprofit's involvement in political activities is evaluated before the nonprofit enters the fray.

Remember, always, that nonprofit organizations are permitted to engage in limited lobbying efforts to advance their missions, but they must not devote a **substantial** part of their activities to influencing

legislation. Moreover, 501(c)(3) organizations are
strictly prohibited from participating in any political
campaign on behalf of or in opposition to a candidate
for public office.

As discussed in chapter 5, nonprofit organizations are
prohibited from participating in political campaigns on
behalf of or against any candidate for public office.
They can, however, still participate in nonpartisan
voter education, registration, and get-out-the-vote
efforts, as long as they remain neutral with respect to
political candidates.

Furthermore, they may engage in limited lobbying
activities, provided these efforts do not comprise a
substantial part of the organization's overall activities.
There are spending limits and technicalities dating
back to the Internal Revenue Code of 1934 that
discourage organizations from spending all of their
time and funding engaged in legislative lobbying.
However, when Congress enacted that legislation,
rather than imposing an absolute ban on all lobbying
by charitable nonprofit organizations they instead set
a limit, providing that, "no substantial part of the
activities" may be for "carrying on propaganda, or
otherwise attempting, to influence legislation."

Thus, while most people (and very many nonprofit organizations) do not realize it, all charitable nonprofits may freely engage in legislative lobbying as long as that activity amounts to only an "insubstantial" amount of the nonprofit's overall activities.

What Does "An Insubstantial Amount" Mean?

The definition of what Congress meant by "an insubstantial" amount has not been described in objective terms by either Congress or the IRS, and the line between an "insubstantial" and a "substantial" amount of legislative lobbying activities is hazy at best, especially because it depends on how the IRS decides to retroactively and subjectively weigh the "facts and circumstances" of each event that comprises legislative lobbying by the nonprofit organization.

Therefore, to avoid the uncertainty of a nonprofit's lobbying activity being measured with this subjective test, we typically recommend that new nonprofits should consider preemptively filing a short one-page form (with a crazy long name): the IRS Form 5768, *Election/Revocation of Election by an Eligible Section 501(c)(3) Organization to Make Expenditures to Influence Legislation*. When a nonprofit organization files this form (also known as "taking the 501(h) election") the organization is electing to be measured by an objective **"expenditure test"** rather than the squishy "substantial" activity and "facts and circumstances" test which is the IRS default.

Filing this Form, and taking the 501(h) election, serves as the most effective "insurance" a nonprofit can secure to protect itself from overstepping IRS limitations on lobbying activities, and putting their exempt status at risk.

Data Privacy, Protection and Security

Data privacy is often thought of as only being important to large, for profit businesses. However, data privacy, protection and security should also be of concern to nonprofit organizations; sometimes it's even more important.

Organizations that handle personal medical data, for example, as part of their data collection and measures of impact must develop and maintain privacy policies and data security protocols to ensure compliance with applicable laws, such as the Health Insurance Portability and Accountability Act (HIPAA) for organizations handling health information, or the General Data Protection Regulation (GDPR) for those with European constituents.

Data privacy generally is defined as a person's ability to determine what, when and how they share their personally identifiable information, and impacts an organization's data storage, collection, and organizational use. That information at issue can vary, but is typically an individual's name, contact information, location, and/or medical information.

Data protection, on the other hand, pertains to **how** your organization will keep personal data safe, follow regulations on data replication, implement mechanisms to protect data loss or failure, and ensure sensitive data is protected from unauthorized access.

Once you've defined the personal data that you need to keep private, and you've determined how best to protect that information, it's time to evaluate how you will keep that data secure. Methods for doing so include monitoring external threats, encryption methodology, authentication protocols to control access, and data loss prevention.

In the United States, there are no national laws in place covering data privacy, like there is in the European Union. The requirements are often very state specific, with statutes varying significantly from one state to another. Since it's such a confusing set of varying rules and regulations, you should research the statutes in effect in your particular state, evaluate the activities you are engaged in, and then determine what you are and what you are not allowed to do with the information you collect.

Insurance

One of the first professionals that a nonprofit founder should seek out (perhaps only after finding an experienced exempt organization's attorney and a nonprofit accountant) is an insurance broker, familiar with the needs of nonprofit organizations.

There are several types of insurance to consider, and the board should consider both when a nonprofit organization is required to purchase insurance, and when it is in the best interest of the organization to purchase elective insurance policies.

Required Insurance

Workers Compensation

A workers compensation insurance policy is required in almost every state for nonprofit organizations with employees. Not only is it required, it's just a really good thing for a purpose-driven organization to implement. After all, coverage for workers' compensation claims will ensure your employees' medical costs and loss of wages for any work-related injuries and illnesses is just the right thing to ensure.

Further, if an employee is injured on the job and thereafter asserts that their injury was caused by unsafe working conditions, the employer will be able to utilize the policy to defend any lawsuits, and typically the policy will include attorneys fees, costs and any settlements or judgments.

Thus, when budgeting for the hiring of employees, remember to factor in workers compensation insurance.

Unemployment Insurance

In all 50 states, all employers - including nonprofit organizations - must pay for unemployment insurance benefits. Typically, this means that they - like any other business - will pay state unemployment insurance taxes. Depending on the state in which your organization operates, unemployment taxes currently range from as little as 0.1 percent to more than 10 percent of each employee's taxable wages, a percentage which can vary from $7,000 to $48,100 per employee.

To add a little complexity, nonprofit organizations also typically have an option that for-profit businesses do not have; instead of paying the tax, they can choose to reimburse the state for any benefits paid out to former employees.

This may sound like a great idea – and it very well may be if you are a large nonprofit employer who can "self-insure." If you're a small nonprofit with only a handful of employees, however, it's important to remember that you will be responsible for all unemployment claims paid to any former employee by the state. Your organization could face a completely unwelcome surprise, owing an unexpectedly large tax bill.

It's important, then, when determining which method to choose that a competent human resources professional "runs the numbers," and can advise you on what the potential liability of selecting the "self-insurance" option could be in the long run.

Elective Insurance

There are other types of insurance available to nonprofit organizations that, while not technically required (unless the organization is subject to a mortgage, lease or lender's requirement), are typically in the best interest of the nonprofit organization and its fiduciaries to consider purchasing. These include directors and officers liability insurance, general liability insurance, property insurance, auto insurance, and employment practices liability insurance.

Directors and Officers Insurance

Often referred to as "D&O" insurance, this type of insurance is meant to protect individuals from personal liability if they are sued in their role as an officer or director of an organization. In essence, this type of insurance protects against the costs of being sued as a result of their service for the organization. While it can cover the individual's errors or omissions, and it can also cover the legal fees and other costs the organization may incur as a result of such a suit, this type of insurance typically does not cover fraud, intentional acts, or criminal activity.

General Liability, Property and Auto Insurance

General Liability Insurance – I typically recommend that the first policy a nonprofit organization should purchase is general liability insurance. It covers against claims made by third parties for bodily injury or property damage that may occur in the course of the nonprofit's operations. Further, you can typically add a Directors and Officers Liability Insurance policy mentioned previously as a "rider" on a general liability policy.

Property or Renters Insurance - Property or renters insurance is pretty self-explanatory, but typically this type of insurance will cover damage or loss to buildings, office equipment, inventory, and any other property the nonprofit rents or owns. It's important to note, however, that basic property or renters insurance policy do not cover floods and earthquakes; additional specialty insurance policies are required if the property is located in a flood or earthquake zone..

Auto Insurance - If the nonprofit organization utilizes automobiles that are used by directors, employees or volunteers they should purchase auto insurance to provide liability coverage including physical damage coverage for those automobiles. Further, nonprofit organizations should also consider non-owned auto insurance coverage for volunteers who use their own vehicles when volunteering for the organization.

Employment Practices Liability Insurance

As discussed in Chapter 5, the biggest risk a nonprofit organization will face will likely be from their decision to become an employer, or to work with volunteers. Defending against a lawsuit from a disgruntled employee alleging sexual harassment, for example, or failure to adequately document and retain personnel records, can cost the organization hundreds of thousands of dollars.

To insure against such a loss, which as you can imagine can be catastrophic to a small nonprofit, insurance companies offer something called "Employment Practices Liability Insurance," or "EPLI."

The cost of obtaining EPLI coverage can be substantial, unfortunately. It largely depends upon what the organization is doing, the number of employees and volunteers the organization has, and whether you've had complaints and allegations of bad employment practices in the past.

Having an EPLI policy can protect the nonprofit organization from bearing the costs of both administrative actions and lawsuits for things like employee discrimination, sexual harassment, wrongful termination, and much more.

In the early days of a nonprofit's lifecycle, most founders discount the risk associated with employing people; after all, you are all committed to the mission of the organization, and the last thing anyone of your passionate volunteers and employees would do is sue you!

Unfortunately, that is simply not the case. In fact, in our experience it seems that the more passionate someone is about something, the more likely they are to seek out an attorney when things don't go "their way."

Let's assume you have an awesome volunteer who has been by your side since you determined you were going to start a new nonprofit organization. You've finally reached the point where you can support a paid position so you advertise for the position, and start interviewing potential employees. The volunteer - let's just call him Joe - applies and he's just not qualified for the position you are seeking to fill, so you hire someone else with more experience. Joe is so passionate about the organization, that he just can not fathom how you could possibly hire anyone else. So, he assumes that he didn't get the position because he's recently disclosed to you that he is gay; so he hires an employment lawyer and sues you.

Even though the lawsuit has no merit, and you know it, you still have to defend the organization against it.

A good policy can cover the organization against employee accusations like Joe's, such as:

- Failure to Hire
- Discrimination
- Wrongful Termination or Discipline
- Retaliation

Depending upon the comprehensiveness of the policy purchased, it could also potentially cover claims related to:

- Breach of an Employment Agreement
- Illegal Background Checks
- Failure to Promote
- Wage and Hour Claims

EPLI typically will cover the legal cost of litigating the case (regardless of whether you win or lose), settlements, or any eventual judgments that are entered related to the employment-related claims. Unfortunately, some agencies will also assess fines and penalties against an employer, and they aren't typically covered under EPLI.

EPLI is typically rather expensive to purchase, and will depend largely on your activities, how many employees, volunteers, or contractors you have, and whether there are any additional risk factors, such as a history of employment-related lawsuits. However, the amount you pay in premiums for EPLI is nothing compared to the expense the organization will incur in defending potential claims.

As an organization just getting started, there's a good chance that you don't have a sophisticated Human Resources professional advising you, yet, so it's important to consider having EPLI protection in case you make a mistake - it happens! - or someone just accuses you of making one (even if you haven't).

Chapter 10 | Culture

> *"This is not about fuzzy, holding hands around a campfire, kumbaya stuff. That's not what values and culture and mission is about.*
>
> *This is about building an organization for success. This is about winning. This is about doing the tactical things to make sure your organization and your people are aligned around the same thing."*
> - Justin Moore

Once you have framed your purpose, your core values, your governance structure and your measures of success, and then have created the right messaging about your programs and your **why**, finding volunteers, potential employees, and the right vendors who support what you've created will likely be easier than you think.

It's time to build your team.

Directors

As described in Chapter 6, it's critically important to frame your organization's governance structure and seek the best directors from the get-go. So, how can you accomplish that task?

Contrary to the highly compensated board members of a public company, the directors of nonprofit organizations typically serve as volunteers, contributing their time because they believe in and support the nonprofit's mission and vision.

Because these types of individuals may not understand, really, what a nonprofit organization is, what the responsibilities of directors are, and what is expected of them and their service, we typically recommend the creation and use of a comprehensive, easy-to-use board orientation manual that board members can use throughout their terms on the board - one that reflects the style of governance you contemplated when reading Chapter 6.

This customized orientation manual provides useful information about the organization, including your board structure and operations, and includes contact information for fellow board members and staff. If consistently used over time, the manual will become an indispensable working tool and a central resource for the director in his or her board service.

Template Director Orientation Manual

We have a free Director Orientation Manual template on our website which we've made available for you to download.

www.nonprofitcounsel.com/start-a-nonprofit-change-the-world-resources

Volunteers

One additional benefit of being recognized as a nonprofit that is tax-exempt under Section 501(c)(3) is an exception to normal wage and hour laws for bona fide volunteers.

The Fair Labor Standards Act (FLSA) establishes minimum wage, overtime pay, record-keeping, and other standards affecting employees in both the nonprofit and business sectors. Under the FLSA, for example, most workers must receive something of value in return for their time and effort in the form of either school credit or wages.

In a nonprofit 501(c)(3), however, volunteer interns, museum docents, tutors or caretakers are the norm.

So how does that work?

Well, in general, an individual will not be considered an employee, subject to minimum wage and hour laws under the FLSA if that individual (1) has volunteered freely to provide labor to fulfill public service, religious or humanitarian objectives; and (2) has no *"contemplation or receipt of compensation."*

Because there should be no compensation provided to a volunteer, nonprofit organizations should be careful about how they appreciate their volunteers, as appreciation made in the form of gift cards, for example, can lead to a perception with tax agencies that the volunteer was actually an employee under the FLSA.

Further, volunteers typically serve on a part-time basis and must not displace regular employees or perform work that would otherwise be performed by those employees. Volunteer labor can be a huge advantage to a growing nonprofit organization, but before launching any volunteer program, you should draft and adopt a comprehensive volunteer manual that clearly describes the restrictions under the FLSA, and consider hiring an attorney to draft a volunteer agreement that includes a release of liability, confidentiality and non-disclosure provisions, a photo release, and an accountable (reimbursement) plan.

Employees

As discussed in Chapter 5, having employees - while necessary to conduct your programs, is often one of the areas of highest risk to any nonprofit employer, whether it's done correctly or not simply because of incredibly strict state employment laws. Thus, it's important to consider some ways to mitigate this potential risk proactively, rather than reactively.

Employment Agreement

In most states, the default is that employment is "at-will." That means that either the employee, or the employer, can decide to terminate the employment relationship with, or without, cause - at any time. In most cases, this ability is in the best interest of both the employer and the employee; providing freedom to the employee to move on, or because the employer finds themselves with an inability to pay the employee's salary.

There are some instances, however, where a nonprofit organization should consider drafting and entering into a formal employment agreement with an employee that contracts around that default. For example, an employment agreement can include a provision requiring advance notice of the employee's resignation, which can serve the purpose of ensuring continuity in either operations or programming.

Employee Handbook

Any new nonprofit organization, prior to hiring its first employee, should consider drafting an employee handbook, a critical tool that will apply to all eventual employees, whenever they are hired. The policies contained in the handbook can serve to mitigate a great deal of the risk related to hiring employees, as it can establish an important part of the employer's defense against a claim of discrimination or harassment. In many states, for example, employers with as few as one employee can be subject to claims of sexual harassment. When an employer fails to have a policy in place that prohibits such harassment, an allegation of wrongdoing can jeopardize the nonprofit organization's ability to defend itself against potential employment related claims.

It's also important when hiring your first employees to consider, for example:

- What is the employee's rate of pay?
- Will they be working part time, or full time? When will they be paid? What will be withheld from their paycheck?
- Are they exempt from receiving overtime pay? (This decision should be based on an analysis of both employment type and salary.)
- What are the legal requirements for offering paid time off? (These requirements can differ by city. In San Diego, California for example, where FPLG is headquartered, accrual for paid

sick time off must be made available to all
employees.)

Just as in a sexual harassment scenario, having a
written employment manual and having policies in
place addressing these issues can serve as a critical
element of any employer's defense against an
employee's claim.

Internal and External Stakeholders

We've already discussed how nonprofit organizations
are different from for-profit businesses; they do not
have "shareholders," who own a piece of the company.
What nonprofit organizations have, however, are
"stakeholders." A stakeholder has an interest in
ensuring the ongoing success of the organization, and
their impact and role in supporting the organization
cannot be overstated.

Donors

In addition to developing great messaging for your
donors, as discussed in Chapter 7, or providing them
with the legally required contemporaneous written
acknowledgment of their contribution as discussed in
Chapter 9, it's important to consider donors as a
critical element of your organization's team and

culture, rather than as simply someone with a fat checkbook.

Remember to invite your donors when you launch a new program, service or team activity. No matter what their giving level, keep them updated and educated on your accomplishments, your challenges and your overall goals. Invitations to appreciation breakfasts, educational seminars that may be of interest to them, or even a small group coffee talk with the board or a group of individuals that have been particularly impacted by your programs can evolve into building a small donor into a lifelong supporter and fan.

Customers and Clients

Many nonprofits appeal to individuals, or offer services to individuals or families. Museums, for example, may have donors - but they likely have a great many more individuals who pay a fee to experience the facility, its educational programs or cultural events; they are your biggest fans because you have impacted them directly.

Don't neglect to consider these individuals as part of your culture, either. They are the ones who experience your service, and broadcast how amazing you are to their friends, family and even random people they meet out on the street. They, too, comprise the overall culture you are building, and will carry your message far and wide.

Professional Services & Vendors

You would likely be surprised to hear me say this, but as an owner of a law firm that supports a great many nonprofit organizations (we have pledged 1% of our revenue to charitable causes), it's been surprisingly difficult in the past for our Culture and Wellness Manager to coordinate volunteer activities and outings for our staff. We seek out opportunities all the time to volunteer our time at fundraising events (we can hand out water to 5k participants all day), but it's way more difficult for us to find those types of opportunities than it should be.

Ask your professional service providers and vendors for support – and not just financial support, or pro bono services. Remember to offer opportunities for these providers to assist and volunteer in ways that are *outside of what they do every day*. For example, our team practices law all day and represents nonprofit clients as part of our profession. When we volunteer, we really want to **get out** into the community, and do something other than the practice of law; we LOVE to volunteer at events, as it's a way we can match our core values and culture with yours.

Give your vendors a chance to become a part of your culture, and you'll have a never ending pipeline of willing volunteers and supporters, and - over time - funding from them very well may follow.

Section 3 | Changing the World

"You have within you the strength, the patience, and the passion to reach for the start to change the world."
- Harriet Tubman

Now that we have covered the five areas of success that every new nonprofit founder should understand, (*Concept, Communications, Cash, Compliance* and *Culture*) it's time to explore what implementing those tools successfully can mean to a new nonprofit organization.

This is the part of the book where you can envision implementing your vision to truly change the world - by learning from those who have already done so.

It's tempting to look around at other organizations and founders and think that there is something special or unique about them, and that you could never be as successful as they are, or make as much of an impact as they have.

But this is simply not the case.

Chapter 11 | Thoughtful Committed Citizens

*"Never doubt that a small group of thoughtful,
committed citizens can change the world;
indeed,
it's the only thing that ever has."*
- Margaret Mead

While the above quote has often been attributed to Margaret Mead the young American anthropologist, it seems that true attribution of this statement by her cannot be definitively substantiated.

Nonetheless, whether it's an actual statement of hers or not, the words are incredibly impactful and demonstrate that the power to change the world, and make a real impact on our communities, lies within each and every one of us.

Beyond the Brotherhood

Sometimes the societal needs that you observe, and that you are uniquely empowered to change, are not those seen by a typical nonprofit founder or even the broader community.

In the fall of 2021, a good friend of mine reached out to ask me to assist in the formation and exemption of a new charitable organization, which he and his co-founders had named *Beyond the Brotherhood*.

Brian Tucker and I had first met over a decade before, when we had both volunteered with our spouses to serve the people of Jamaica and Guatemala by providing health and medical services in the poorest of communities. Since that initial service together, we had worked on behalf of various charitable organizations, both large and small, but he knew that this new endeavor was a little different.

Beyond the Brotherhood sought to serve one of the strongest, and yet most underserved, communities in the United States: former US Navy SEALs. These individuals are not what anyone would picture when thinking of someone needing help, but Brian and his co-founders had observed an unmet need, utilizing the preception discussed early on in this text, and they believed that they were in a position to make a huge difference in the lives of these highly-trained warriors.

They had observed that despite an incredible level of strength, extensive set of skills, and military education, SEALs transitioning out of the military are often lacking support and guidance. They are frequently not well prepared to navigate civilian life, as the intensive pace and confidential nature of their work as a SEAL often prevents them from forging the kind of social connections and professional networks that are commonplace to all of us, and necessary to succeed professionally in their career.

Further, Brian had been diligently working for almost two decades to build his business enterprise, *Punta Brava*, and his vision for Beyond the Brotherhood included a close relationship with his business enterprise. This close relationship required a careful analysis of both the private benefit and commerciality doctrines.

So Brian picked up the phone and gave me a call to determine how best to proceed with this new enterprise as a nonprofit 501(c)(3) tax exempt organization.

Over the next nine months, we worked together to efficiently establish the organization. They outsourced their formation, exemption and initial charity registration paperwork to For Purpose Law Group (FPLG), allowing the founders to focus on developing their *concept*, crafting their *communications* strategy, focusing on their *cash*, and instituting their organizational *culture*.

You might have noticed that one of the featured components of this book, "*compliance*," was omitted. Due to the complexities of the close relationship between *Punta Brava* and *Beyond the Brotherhood*, they have outsourced much of their legal compliance to FPLG as well, asking us to assist them in the role of "Outside General Counsel." In this capacity, the entire FPLG team is on standby for the organization, poised and ready to provide relevant guidance, and is available in case the organization encounters any legal issues or compliance challenges.

Visit: www.BeyondtheBrotherhood.org to view their compelling video case for support, conveying their purpose and inviting others to join them.

Last accessed June 2023.

Boulder Creek Research Institute

In June of 2022, I had an initial consultation with Stephen W. Evans, the founder of Boulder Creek Research Institute (BCRI). He reached out to ask for our assistance in forming a new nonprofit research institute.

After serving as a medic in the army for five years, Stephen's career had been cut short due to injuries. However, his experiences during that time ignited a deep fascination with the brain and the workings of human cognition.

During his pursuit of a PhD, Stephen observed the increasingly cutthroat nature of academic careers in neuroscience. To secure a tenure-track research faculty position at a university, scientists must possess a PhD, but they must also excel in post-doctoral fellowships, which often required neuroscientists to relocate anywhere in the country or even the world, disrupting their family and community ties. Working 60+ hours a week until tenure, scientists endure low pay and adverse living conditions, making it challenging to start a family until quite late in life.

The resulting scientific landscape is one of overworked, stressed, and underpaid researchers detached from their communities. Teaching and outreach efforts suffer, as scientists struggle to find time to engage with students and convey their passion for neuroscience effectively.

Stephen believed that there was a better way. He knew he could build a research institute that could give talented people the time to build relationships outside of work, and outside of science. This would serve to maintain family and community stability, as well as increase the quality of teaching while reaching historically underserved populations without access to this level of educational instruction.

Thus, BCRI was born. Stephen's vision for BCRI is that the organization's approach will inspire institutions to reconsider their scientific practices and foster a more supportive and inclusive environment for researchers.

When seeking assistance in establishing BCRI, Stephen considered navigating the process himself. However, he recognized the complexity and time-consuming nature of the legal aspects involved, and he understood that the legal foundation would shape the long-term future success of the nonprofit.

After we completed all of the steps required, he mentioned that he chose FPLG to handle the legal aspects of establishing BCRI largely due to reading our positive reviews online. According to Stephen, the experience exceeded his expectations, as FPLG made the process "easy and streamlined," relieving Stephen of the burden of paperwork and formalities, so that he could focus on what truly mattered – advancing neuroscience research and making a positive impact in his community.

Based on his experience in founding a new organization, Stephen advises nonprofit founders to "have a clear and achievable vision," and to identify the goals they hope to accomplish, first. He also shared his belief that it's equally crucial to surround oneself with the right people, as a supportive and competent team will contribute to the overall success of the organization.

Pathway to Kinship

The above stories might lead you to believe that everything always goes well, and there are no failures or missteps along the way. I wish I could confirm that assumption, but as Henry Ford once observed, *"Obstacles are those frightful things you see when you take your eyes off your goal."*

Over the past 150 or so pages of this book, I've featured when things go right from the start. But what happens when you realize that choices made early on in the process have been a mistake?

Marc Vahanian's vision is to help people get free, and stay free. The organization that he founded, *Pathway to Kinship*, works to make the journey to freedom and re-entry into society possible for people who have been incarcerated by offering housing, education and employment counseling and resources.

> *"We see resilient and purposeful formerly incarcerated citizens who are able to re-invent themselves and become contributing members of our society. We see people who have many ways to be of service and so much to offer."*

At the very beginning of Pathway to Kinship in January of 2022, Marc chose to work with a well-known online service to start the process. He believed that a service that is the biggest self-help "legal" service in the world must be the best available option to take care of the paperwork, and to ensure that his new organization was set up correctly and poised for growth.

He then turned his eyes to building his program and services, having faith that everything else would be completed by the online service he had paid to do so..

It didn't take long for Marc to become disappointed with the lack of support and guidance offered by this particular "legal" behemoth. When he reached out to FPLG in March of 2022, he described the relationship as challenging, and that they "failed to deliver," and the service was "not as advertised."

During our initial consultation, Marc was frustrated that several months had passed since he decided to work with this particular company, and during that time he was not only distracted from the work he could have been accomplishing within the community, but he was struggling to get things completed that should have been handled at the very beginning of the process.

Ultimately, he chose to engage with FPLG and we were able to quickly "pick up the baton," complete the process of formation and exemption, and provide the necessary and relevant guidance he needed to begin the work he wished to accomplish. When we recently asked him about his experience, he noted: "We called various attorneys and found very few who specialized in *working with nonprofits. May answered all my questions, made clear and upfront how the fees for the services would work. And then she and her team delivered as promised."*

The reason I am including Marc's experience in this book is because mistakes and missteps do happen, but it's **never too late** to recalibrate, solve the issue, and get back on track. Do not let initial obstacles and failures derail you and your organization; there are resources out there that are available to you that can get you back on track.

When asked what he would share of the path he has taken, and the experiences he had in forming a new nonprofit organization to other nonprofit founders, Marc provides the following advice.

> *Have a definite purpose. Know the arena you want to participate in; be specific about how and who you wish to impact.*
>
> *Expand your circle of advisors. Speak to other people who are already successful in the space. Identify organizations that have struggled and find out why.*

Do your due diligence and prepare yourself for the endless array of things that can and will go wrong.

Starting and implementing your own nonprofit is a major mental, emotional, physical and spiritual undertaking. It helps to have faith, friends and funding.

Keep the faith!

Visit: www.PathwaytoKinship.org to view their compelling video case for support, conveying their purpose and inviting others to join them.

Last accessed June 2023.

Conclusion

In the pages of this book I have endeavored to share not only theoretical "how-to" guidance with you, but also to provide practical real-world advice, drawing from my experience in advising countless nonprofit organizations over the past two decades.

My hope is that I have empowered you with the confidence and the strategic knowledge that will be necessary for you to navigate the complexities of the process successfully.

During our journey together, we have explored the fundamental legal tenets of nonprofit organizations, and have covered the crucial aspects that should be considered when starting and leading a nonprofit organization.

We began by exploring the concept of "preception," recognizing that nonprofit founders have the unique gift of envisioning change, and orchestrating how they can bring that change to fruition.

Then, we identified the path that leads to success by defining the organization's compelling mission, and the time-well-spent in devising a strategic plan to achieve it. As part of that path to success, we explored the critical communications strategies that can be utilized, including finding your organization's "why" and developing your case for support.

Then, we navigated the challenges of understanding the required legal structure and establishing a strong financial foundation. We evaluated the risk while surveying the complex federal and state compliance regulations facing nonprofit organizations, including the operational considerations that underpin the smooth operations of a well-founded nonprofit organization.

Finally, we've discussed how critical it is to assemble a high-caliber team, and to diligently build your unique culture as you move forward.

Throughout this odyssey, I have sought to share real-world examples and to share various lessons I, and others, have learned along the way.

Remember that this path need not be traversed alone. Nurture connections with fellow nonprofit leaders, forge collaborations, and harness the collective wisdom and support that are available to you. Find your tribe! It is through these connections that you will be able to achieve and surpass the expectations you have set for yourself.

You have immense power that lies at your fingertips— the power to effect profound change, uplift communities, and shape a brighter future for us all.

May you inspire, uplift, and ignite the flames of change wherever you venture! The world lies within your capable hands.

Next Steps

I hope this book has sparked some new thinking and new insights for you, and provided to you the roadmap mentioned in the Introduction. Whenever you're ready, here are three ways we can help:

1. Subscribe to the Nonprofit Podcast.
    www.NonprofitCounsel.com/podcast.

2. Subscribe to FPLG's amazing Nonprofit Insights, full of relevant nonprofit information.
    www.FPLGLaw.com/Insights

3. Work with For Purpose Law Group when you need legal, accounting or tax assistance.
    Just send us an email at
    clientsolutions@forpurposelaw.com to see if we are a good fit to work together!

4. Check out Nonprofit Counsel for educational resources and courses of interest to nonprofit founders, leaders and board members, and sign up for our email newsletter. We'll be continually adding courses, webinars and other resources that you may find useful.

About the Author

May L. Harris, Esq., M.A.
Founder | CEO of For Purpose Law Group (FPLG)
Founder | CEO of Nonprofit Counsel

May L. Harris, Esq., M.A. is an attorney who possesses a deep commitment to serving nonprofit organizations, and she is well-versed in the complex legal intricacies that govern their operations. This expertise enables her to provide invaluable guidance, ensuring compliance and helping nonprofits navigate legal challenges with confidence.

Beyond her legal practice, Ms. Harris holds a Master of Arts degree in Nonprofit Leadership and Management, and she understands the challenges facing nonprofit leaders every day, and has dedicated her life's work to advising nonprofit tax-exempt organizations, helping them to establish, protect and fulfill their mission, vision and values.

Acknowledgments

A huge thank you to the hundreds of nonprofit leaders who have had faith in me and the For Purpose Law Group team over the past twenty years. Not only have I learned so much from each and every one of you, but I treasure being a part of your passion and your path in changing our world for the better.

To my colleagues at For Purpose Law Group, for dedicating their professional careers to the support of our nonprofit clients, showing the world that attorneys and law firms **do** have hearts; really **big** ones.

To my father, for demonstrating an entrepreneurial spirit and kickstarting my decision to go to law school, even while I was a new mom with a toddler in tow.

To my mother, for showing me what a strong and independent woman could accomplish with love, hard work, and dedication.

To Cameron and Haley, my awesome kiddos, for inspiring me to be a lifelong learner alongside you.

And finally to my husband Eric, for being my biggest cheerleader... you've never faltered in your faith in my ability to do whatever I set my mind to. **You are my person**, and I couldn't do any of this without your support.

Made in the USA
Las Vegas, NV
15 February 2024

85834937R00111